STUDIES ON BUDDHIST MONASTERIES IN LADAKH
(A Case of Matho Monastery of Sakya Order)

STUDIES ON BUDDHIST MONASTERIES IN LADAKH

(A Case of Matho Monastery of Sakya Order)

Dr. Prem Singh Jina

CYBER TECH PUBLICATIONS
4264/3, Ansari Road, Daryaganj, New Delhi-110002 (India)
Ph.: 011-23244078, 011-43559448 Fax: 011-23280028
E-Mail: cyberpublicationsdelhi@yahoo.com
Website: www.cybertechpublications.com

STUDIES ON BUDDHIST MONASTERIES IN LADAKH

Prem Singh Jina

First Edition 2011

Published by :

G.S. Rawat for **Cyber Tech Publications**
4264/3, Ansari Road, Daryaganj, New Delhi-110002 (India)
Ph.: 011-23244078, 011-43559448 Fax: 011-23280028
E-Mail: cyberpublicationsdelhi@yahoo.com
Website: www.cybertechpublications.com

Dedicated to

Mrs. Manju Jina & Manu

Contents

Preface

Ladakh is a centre of Mahayana Buddhism, may be called little Tibet in India. It has all the major sect monasteries viz., Geluk-pa, Nyingma-pa, Sakya-pa and Ka'gyud pa. I choose Matho this time, as no research work on this monastery is conducted to the best of my knowledge. I made several visits since April 2006 to the monastery and did research work at my own expenses. Finally, the monograph ready for publication. .I hope my this effort will fulfil the basic requirements of Research scholars, teachers and tourists of the world, who want to know about the details of Matho monastery of Ladakh.

Dr. Prem Singh Jina

Email: psjina@gmail.com

Acknowledgements

I would like to express deep appreciation to Dr. (Mrs.) Kapila Vatsayayan, chairperson, India International Centre, 40 Max Muller Marg, New Delhi, who always ready to help me as and when required.

I would fail in performing my moral duties if I forget to mention Mrs. Manju Jina, Principal, Hira Convent School, Haldwani (Uttrakhand), who helped me in various ways in completing this book.

I am also greateful to Matho monastery Lamas, Rev Nawang Thokmet and authors by whose thought and works, I have benefited immensely.

At the end I am grateful to Shri Kripal D. Joshi, a Delhi-based Editor, who has been instrumental in the publication of this book well in time.

Dr. Prem Singh Jina

Email: psjina@gmail.com

1

Origin and Growth of Sakya Order

The beginning of linege of Sa-kya (Sakya) tradition is rooted in an interesting story which relates that in olden days three brothers, known as the "gods of clear light" descended to earth. Thereafter they had established their relationship with demons in Tibet. During those days people of Tibet did not have good relationship with them. However, to a demon and a married woman, a divine son was born, who later known Jo bo khon par skyes (Pron. Chowo Khon Parskye), meaning the "Lord Born Amidst quarrels." He was the ancestor of the noble Khon family. His son "khon dpal po che" was a historical person, and his son' Khon Kluhi dbang po became the disciple of Padmasambhava. Later he became one of the seven sad-mi or "tested men" as the first seven monks of the Tibetan monastic system. In this way 'Khon Kluhi dbang po later known rdorje rinpoche gave birth to Sa-kya tradition in Tibet.[1]

Unfortunately during 9th Century Langdarma persecuted Buddhism, as a result Khon family who were the centre of Sa-kya tradition scattered. However, one family member of Khon named Sakya Lodro (Tib. Sa-kya blo gros), again thought to re-establish Sa-kya tradition. He had two sons Shes rab tshal khrims and 'Khon dkon mchog rgyal po. They later became monks. Khon mchog rgyal po studied under Tibetan scholar Drokmi. In 1073 he founded Sa-kya monastery at the Grum River bank 94 km southwest of Xigaze. Thereafter, it became the centre establishment and seat of power, subsequently the name of the Buddhist tradition named Sa-kya pa after the Sa-kya monastery.[2]

Kon mchog rgyal po married very late at the age of fifty nine. He had a son, who later named kunga snying po. He was born in 1092. He collected hundreds of sutras and tantras as well as oral instructions and recognized as an authoritative expounder of Sa-kya tradition. He had four sons (Table 1.1). The three sons devoted themselves to religion. The youngest as dpal chen' od po had two sons viz, kunga Gyal mtshan and Zangs tsha bsod nams rgyal mtshan, kunga Gyal mtshan, popularly known Sakya Pandita. He entered religious life and became the abbot of Sakya, later through his profound knowledge about Buddhism known as Sakya Pandita, meaning "the learned scholar of Sakya order.[3]

TABLE 1.1

Family Tree of Sakya Pandita

'Khon dkon mchog rgyal po (khon konchok Gyalpo(1034-1102)

Kun dga' snying po (kunga Nyingpo (1092-1158)

(1) Kun dga' bar

(2) bsod nams rtsemo

(3) grags pa rgyal mtshan

(4) dpal chen-'od po

(1) Kun dga rgyal mtshan (Sa-kya pandita)

(2) Zangs tsha bsod nams rgyal-mtsan

(1) 'phagspa blo grs rgyal mtsan

(2) phyag na rdo rje (chang Dorje)

The above table reveals that dpal chen od po and Zangtsha bsod nams rgyal mtshan continued the family line of Sa-kya tradition. Zangtsha bsod nams rgyal mtshan had five wives and seven children. In brief, it can be concluded that Sakya tradition was strengthened by five scholars.[4]

(1) kun dga 'snying po (Kunga NBying po)
(2) bsod nams rtse mo
(3) grags pa rgyal mtshan

(4) kun dga' rgyal mtshan (Sakya Pandita)
(5) 'Phags pa blo gros rgyal mtshan.

Sakya Pandita (or kun dga rgyal mtshan) and his two nephews 'phags pa and phag na rdo rje played an important role to establish close relation with Mongolia.[5] Sakya Pandita left Sakya in 1244 along with his nephews. In 1247 he met prince Godan. He remained at the court of Godan, established good relationship with Mongols, and died in Mongolia in 1251. After some time King of Mongolia Godan also died. The Mongolian empire then divided between the two brothers—Mangu and Kublai. In 1259 both brothers jointly campaigned against China. In this war Mangu died. Kublai Khan was elected his successor in 1260. He later became the emperor of China and in 1271 his dynasty named Ta Yuan. In 1279 he brought entire .China under the Mongol rule.[6]

After the death of Sakya Pandita his nephew 'phags pa became the leading figure of Sa-kya tradition. He influenced Kublai Khan. Later by his efforts he was converted to Buddhism. He conferred upon him the title of Hevajra. Buddhism thereafter became the national religion of his kingdom. 'phags pa was appointed national preceptor. Kublai khan even offered him three regions of Tibet. Thus phags pa had spiritual authority over the entire kingdom of Kublai Khan. In the Kublai kingdom Kublai Khan and phags pa relationship was so close as people then called them like sun and the moon in the sky.[7]

'phags pa's brother phyag na rbo-rje by the time became dpon-chen had central administrative power of Mongolian empire. He married with Godan Khan's daughter and Kublai's daughter. He died at an young age of 29 years in 1267 with the high standing of the Sakya tradition. Phagspa in 1265 went to Tibet to review the activities of his tradition in Tibet, however after four years returned to China. In 1276 he again went to Sakya. By the time there emerged a thought in Tibet that with the influence of Sakya tradition in administration, the activities of other sects might be hampered. But phags pa did not bother. With this sort of misunderstanding, he held a Great Council in 1280. He did not know the above rumour very well and was died under suspect.[8]

Therefore by the grace of 'phags pa Sakya tradition had strong hold in the whole Mongolian empire including Tibet. But after his death Sakya doctrine did not last long. Phag mo gru pa defeated Sakya-pa. However, Sa-kya pa continued to establish good relations with phag mo gru pa, and the related monastery named as Sa kya gdan sa.[9]

The member of the lang family who led the revolt and founded the political power of the Phagmogru-pa was Changchup Gyal mtshan. In 1354 he defeated Sakya pa and emerged as the effective ruler. He maintained a strenuous relationship with Yuan Dynasty. In 1368 the last emperor of the Yuan Dynasty was driven out of China and founded Ming Dynasty by a Buddhist monk. However, Changchup Gyal mtshan and his successors, a series of some eleven Lamas of the Phagmogru-pa lineage ruled the land from 1354 to 1435.[10]

Thus from 1354 onwards political change took place in China and its adjoining regions. Likewise changes also taken in the Sakya tradition, and a number of branches emerged such as:

(i) Sakya
(ii) Ngor
(iii) Tsar
(iv) Bulug/Shalu
(v) Jonang
(vi) Jonang Taranatha
(vii) Bodong
(viii) Dzongpa

These lineage are based upon Sakya Pandita Teachings.

Ngorchen Kunga Zangpo (1382-1457) and his successors Kunchok Lundrup, Thartse Namkha Chimed Palzang and Drubkhang Paldan Dondup founded Ngor lingeage.

Tsarchen Losal Gyatso (1502-56), followed by Jamyang khyantse Wangchuk and Mangthos Lundrup Gyatso founded Tsar lineage.

The other roots of Sakya lineages viz. Bulug/shalu founded by Button Thamchat khyenpa. Jonang tradition founded by Dolpopa sherab Gyaltsan. The Jonang Taranatha and Bodong traditions founded by Bodong Panchen Choglas Namgyal. Finally the Dzongpa was founded by Dzongpa kunga namgyal.

All the above lineages of Sakya order home only a minor differences according to the theories of Sutra and tantras.

In Ladakh Sakya order started spreading from 13th century. Later in 1414 A.D. Tung pa Dorje arrived Matho village near Leh. Dragspa Bumde was then the king of Ladakh, subsequently by his patronage he built a Lhakhang in Matho, later developed as Matho monastery.

In conclusion Sakya pa had strong hold during 11th to 13th Century A.D. throughout in China, Mongolia and Tibet. In 1334 Phagmogru pa emerged as politically more powerful. However Sakya and Ngor Sakya traditions were remain popular in Tibet. In Ladakh lamas from Matho monastery were used go to Sakya and Ngor monasteries for higher studies. In 1959 Tibet was occupied by China, this tradition thus stopped. Today lamas from this monastery go to Dehradun, Uttrakhand for higher studies.

NOTES AND REFERENCES

1. Finegan Jack: *Tibet : A Dreamt of Image,* Tibet House and Wiley Eastern Ltd., New Delhi, 1986, p. 88.
2. *Ibid.*
3. *Ibid.*, p. 105.
4. The five great Sakya scholars are known 'Gongma Nga. They hold an important place in the Sakya tradition. Sachen kunga Nyingpa Tib. (Kun dga, snying pa 1092-1158) is recognised as the first 'Gongma'. He was the son of khon Konchok Gyalpo (1034-1102) and was an eminent scholar of Sakya order. He collected hundred of sutra, tantras and oral instructions. This collection later became the basis of Sakya order Lobpon Sonam Tsemo (Tib. Bsod nams rtse mo) and Jetsun Dakpa Gyaltsen (Tib. Grags pa rgyal mtshan) are the second and third 'Gongma'. They through their teachings and meditation enhanced the activities of Sakya order. Sakya Pandita kunga Gyaltsan (1182-1251) was the most famous scholar of Sakya order and recognised as the fourth Gongma. During his period Sakya tradition spread its firmed roots in China and Mongolia. Chogyal Phakpa (1235-1280) succeeded him as the fifth Gongma. During his period Sakya school of Philosophy and tradition reached its political zenith, with the introduction of Mahayana Buddhism into China

and Mongolia. The Mongol ruler Kublai Khan in devotion offered the thirteen myriachies of Tibet to him. Thus Tibet was united under a joint spiritual and political authority. These five masters are known as 'Jetsun Gongpa Nga' and are considered as the real founder of Sakya tradition. Cf. H.H Sakya Trizin: *A Brief History of the Sakya Tradition in Mangtro Monastery;* Janyang Gyaltsan (ed).; Cultural and Welfare Society Mangtro, Gonpa Leh, 2005 pp. 6-7.

5. Phagspa was the first person in Tibetan history gain religious and secular authority over the entire country. It was the period when the Lhakang Chhenmo was constructed Sakya. He was succeeded by his brother Chana Dorje and altogether Sakyapas ruled Tibet for more than a hundred years. Eventually Tashi kunglo (1299-1327) eldest of fifteen grandson of Sakya Pandita's brother founded four dynastic palaces (Phodrang); Zhıthog, Rinchen Gang, Lhakhang and Ducho of which only the last survives. In the eighteenth Century at the time of Sakya trizin Wangdu Nyingpo the second Padmasambhava of this age, the Ducho palace split into two; The Dolma phodrang and Phuntsok phodrang. The present head of the Sakya tradition the 41st holder of Sakya throne is living in Dehradun (Uttarakhand), India. His Holiness has two sons, Ratna Vajra and Gyana Vajra. He has also a sister, Jesunma Chimey Luding who teaches extensively throughout the world. Gongma Dagchen Rinpoche of the Phuntsok palace founded Sakya, Thegchen Chosling in Seattle, wash, U.S.A. He had one brother Gongma Thinly Rinpoche a monk who passed away recently. Dagchen Rinpoche also has five sons. The second son Ananda Vajra Rinpoche an accomplished lawyer is assisting the Dalai Lama and the Tibetan refuge government with legal and constitutional matters. Succession to the position of Sakya Trizin head of the Sakya tradition has been hereditary since the time of khon Konchok Gyalpo and recently alternates between the two palaces. Cf. H.H. Sakya Trizin, *op. cit.*, p. 13.
6. Finegan Jack; *op. cit.*, 109.
7. *Ibid.*
8. *Ibid.*, 110.
9. *Ibid.*, 111
10. *Ibid.*, 111-112.

2

Sakya Philosophy and Teachings

Indian great Acharyas and learned scholars made an important contribution for sutra and tantra of Buddhism. Later Sakya scholars assimilated the same into the spiritual life of Tibet. The most famous of these are: The Hevajra tantras whose transmission with the Mahasidha Virupa the Vajrakila tantras of Padmasambhva the Vajrayogini precepts of Naropa. The Guhyasamaja Tantra teaching of Nagarjuna and the Mahakala precepts of Vararuci. Yogin Gyadhara later propagated Buddhist tantra in Tibet. He was the teacher of Drokmi, Sakya scholars belief in the Philosophy "Non-differentiation of Samsara and Nirvana" and it posits of "Non-dual luminosity-emptiness" beyond all extremes. In terms of spiritual teaching the Sakya masters have always stressed, in study and meditation like measure. This ideal so teachers has won respect for the Sakya tradition as one not only of learned scholars but of enlightened sages. The Sakya tradition has the distinction of leaving a close connection with the Nyingma, Ka'gyud and Gelukpa tradition from guru Padmasambhava the founder of Nyingmapa, Sakya scholars learned Vajrakila Tantra, Vajrayogini from Naropa, Tsongkhapa, the founder of Gelukpa order, studied under many Sakya Lamas such as Rendwa Shonnu Lodos. In this way Sakya tradition correlated with other major Buddhist tradition of Mahayana and developed accordingly through the ages.[1]

It is said that in the eleventh century one of the head of the family. Sherab Tsultrim of Tang region decided to seek new Tantra from India. In those days Padmasambhava Tantric tradition was very much popular in India. Guru Padmasambhava wrote: "An emanation of the Indian Virupa- Drokmi Lotsava will appear."

The younger brother, konchok Gyalpo, went to study with Drokmi Lotsava (992-1074). At an auspicious location, below a white patch of earth (Sa-Kya), Prophesied by Guru Padmasambhva and Atisa, Khon Konchok Gyalpo built the first temple Gorum Zimci Karpo in 1073 A.D. This marks the beginning of Sakya tradition. The holy family, the hereditary leaders of this precious lineage are known by three names:[2]

(i) Lha Rig
(ii) Khon
(iii) Sakya.

Sachan kunga Nyingpo (1092-1158), the son of Khon konchok Gyalpo, had extraordinary skill and spiritual attainment, studied various Sutra and tantra. He got teachings on Vajrakila and Samputa from khon konchok Gyalpo. Later he practised the same. He received teaching on Chakrasamvara, Guhyasamaj Vajra Bhairava etc. from Bari, Lotsava. He studied Lamdre system, Samayogadakinijala and other Mahayani Tantric systems from Shangton Chobar for four years; received teachings on Chakrasamvara, Bhairava, Vajrayogini and Panjarnatha Mahakala from Mal Lotsava Ledro Drag. Finally he received the instructions on outer inner and secret of four faced protector Caturmukha from Lama Nam khapa.[3]

Sachan kunga Nyingpo also received Lamders teachings from Shangton and directly from Virupa in a series of visions that lasted a month. This is known 'Recent' or 'close' Lamdre lineage.[4]

Sachan kunga Nyingpo had four sons:

(i) Kunga Bar (Tib. Kun dga' bar)
(ii) Sonam tsemo (bsod nam rtse mo 1142-1182)
(iii) Trakpa Gyaltsan (Tib. Grags pa rgyal mtshan (1147-1216)
(iv) Palchen Odpo (Tib. Dpal chen od po 1150-1203).

All the above studied Buddhist philosophy and tantra under different Indian scholars. Kunga Bar studied Buddhist Philosophy in Nalanda university, but died soon. The second son Sonam tsemo became a learned scholar at an early age of sixteen. At the age of forty-one he ascended bodily Khecara the divine realm of Vajra Yogini. He had visions of many meditional deities and also produced many realised disciples. Trakpa Gyaltsan received celibacy vows and showed strong signs of spiritual maturity in his youth. At the age of eleven he gave his first Heavajra teachings.[5]

The fourth son Palchen Odpo (or Palchen OdPochey) had two sons kunga Gyentsen (Pron. Sakya Pandita) and Sangtha Sonam Gyentsen. Sakya pandita was a famous Sakya scholar, he studied Buddhist and Non-Buddhist philosophical texts, books, Tantra, Logic. Sanskrit poetry, Astrology and art with many Indian, Nepalese, Kashmiri and Tibetan Masters. Subsequently achieved mastery over all those subjects.

At the age of 27 years he became a fully ordained monk after meeting with Kashmiri Pandita Shakya Shribhadra. His famous works are 'Treasury of Logic on Valid Cognition (Tib. Tsad-ma rigster) and 'Discrimination of the Three Vows (Tib. sdon-gsun–rab-dbye). He wrote 114 religious treatises. The treasury of Logic on Valid Cognition (Tib. Tsad-ma- rigs- ster)' was the only text of Tibetan origin ever to have been translated into Sanskrit. The translation was rendered by his Indian students at Nalanda University and was received with much acclaim.[6]

The heart of the Sakya tradition is Lamders (Tib. lam bras), the path and its result one of the most comprehensive and systematically organized meditative system of tantric Buddhism. As said earlier the basic tantric tradition received by Sakyapa by Mahasidha Virapa. The same later continued down through Indian Mahasiddhas and Tibetan translation the great masters of the Sakya tradition. At the time of Muchen sempa chenpo konchok Gyaltsan, a disciple of Ngorchen kunga Zangpo, Lamdre was divided into two:[7]

(i) The uncommon teaching (Tib. Slob-bshad)
(ii) The common teaching (Tib. Tshog- bshad).

The philosophical viewpoint expressed in the path and its result in the 'Non-differentiation of Samsara and Nirvana' and the 'Inseparability of clarity and emptiness.' Therefore an individual cannot attain nirvana by abandoning samsara (cyclic existence), because the mind is the root of both sansara and nirvana. When obscured, it takes the form of sansara and when freed of oscurations it is Nirvana. Hence, the reality is that a person must strive through meditation realise their inseparability.[8]

Sakya tradition is based upon various group of lineages viz.[9]

(i) Group of four Tantras : Hevajra Chakrasamvara, Guhyasamaja and Vajra Bhairava

(ii) Thirteen Golden Dharmas are:
   (a) Three Red Ones
   (b) Three Great Red Ones
   (c) Three Lesser Red Ones
   (d) Black Manjusri
   (e) Avalokitesvara Simhanda
   (f) Sabala Garuda
   (g) Red Jambhala.

There are several different versions of emanation in all the above sets. The three sets of Red ones have received consistent. These are the main Anuttara Yoga tantric practice of Sakya order.[10]

At present Sakya teachings are taught at only a few colleges. The main is in Rajpura, Dehradun (Uttarakhand), and the other is in Boudhanath in Kathmandu, Nepal. A few still remain in Tibet such as Dzongsar khamje Ling. According to Sakya order eighteen texts deal with the perfection of wisdom, Monastic discipline (Vinaya), Madhyamika view, Phenomenology, Logic and epistemology, besides, Sakya Pandita's Discrimination of three views and the treasury of Logic on valid cognition and Goranpa Sonams Senga works are also important. After completing their studies in the Sakya colleges monks are granted Kazhipa, Kachupa and Rabjampa degree on the basis of merit.[11]

The major Sakya monasteries in Central Tibet are:[12]

(i) Lhakhang Chenmo : Founded by khan Konchok Gyalpo

(ii) Ngor Ewam Choden : Founded by Ewam Kunga Zangpo

(iii) Dar Drangmoche in Tsang : Founded by Tsarchen Losal Gyatso (Tsarpa main monastery

(iv)	Nalanda in Phen Po	: Founded & built by Rongton Shesa kunrig
(v)	Tsedong Sisum Namgyal	: Founded and built by Namkha Tashi Gyaltsan
(vi)	Dhondup Ling in khan province	: Founded by Dagchen Sherab Gyaltsan
(vii)	Dzongsar	: Jamyang khyentse Wangpo
(viii)	Deur chode in Amdo	: Founded and built by Chodak Sangpo
(ix)	Tsechem stanpai Gatsal in Rajpura Dehradun (Uttarakhand)	: Sakya monastery
(x)	Sa Magaon in Himachal Pradesh (India)	: Sakya monastery
(xi)	Ngor Ewam chosldan in Manduwala, Dehradun (Uttarakhand)	: Ngorpa monastery
(xii)	Tashi Rabten Ling at Lumbini	: Tsarpa lineage
(xiii)	Matho in Matho Village near Leh (Ladakh)	—
(xiv)	Lhundrup Teng of Dege Funded by Thangtong Gryalpo	

Besides the above there are many small Sakya monasteries in China, Mongolia, Western Tibet, Nepal and India.

At present his holiness Sakya Trizin Ngawang kunga is the head of Sakya school. Luding khan Rinpoche, is the head of the ngor school and Chogye trichen Rinpoche is the head of the tsarpa school.[13]

In conclusion, Sakya tradition is based upon four major tantras viz. Hevajra, Chakrasamvara, Guhyasamaj and Vajra Bhairava. The other prominent lineages help practitioner to achieve perfection of wisdom.

NOTES AND REFERENCES

1. H.H. Sakya Trizin: *A Brief History of the Sakya Tradition,* In : Mangtro Monastery' Jamyang Gyaltsan (ed) Cultural and Welfare Society, Mangtro Gonpa, Leh, 2005, pp. 7-8.
2. *Ibid.*, p. 9.
3. *Ibid.*, pp. 9-10.

4. *Ibid.*, p. 13.
5. *Ibid.*, p. 11.
6. *Ibid.*
7. *Ibid.*, p. 15.
8. *Ibid.*
9. *Ibid.*, p. 16.
10. *Ibid.*
11. *Ibid.*
12. *Ibid.*, pp. 16-17.
13. *Ibid.*, p. 17.

3

High Ranked Lamas Who Visited Matho Monastery

Since the 15th Century A.D. onwards Matho monastery was visited by high ranked Lamas of Sakya tradition. In the 15th century Dorjė Palzang established Sakya monastery at Matho Village, near Leh. Thereafter in order to strengthen this tradition time and again many Sakya scholars visited the site and made their valuable contribution to the preservation and propagation of Sakya tradition in Ladakh. Here follows a list of such scholars of Sakya order who visited the monastery.[1]

1. drung chen rdo rje dpal bzang : In 15th century, he visited Matho village, later established a Sakya temple there. The same was developed as Matho monastery of Sakya tradition, the only and main monastery of this tradition in Ladakh.
2. drung pa bsod nams blo gros: He refounded the monastery after renovation of old and ruined temples.
3. drung pa bsod sras.
4. mkhan chem blo gros rgya mtso
5. drung pa mkan po
6. drung pa shes rab legs pa
7. drung pa rgya mtso
8. drung pa kun dg'a rgyal mtsan
9. bla ma chos kyi blo gros
10. bla ma kun dg'a dpal ldan
11. bla ma bsod nams blo gros
12. bla ma dkon mchog bstan' ajin
13. bla ma dpal ldan ' aphrin las

14. bla ma' aphrin las bk'a bbas
15. bla ma lhun grub chos aphel
16. bla ma' shakya bzang po
17. bla ma' aphrin las phun tsogs
18. bla ma' kun dg'a brtson' agrus
19. bla ma' achi med rdo rje mam rgyal
20. bla ma' rgyal sras phun tsogs rnam rgyal
21. Klu lding mkhan po' ajam dbyangs-bstan p'ai nyi ma[2]
22. Klu lding mkhan po' ajam dbyangs chos kyi rgyal mtsan.

REFERENCES

1. Jamyang Gyaltsan : *Mangtro monastery,* Culture Welfare Society, Mangtro Gonpa, Leh; 119-20
2. Klu lding mkhan poajam - ·dbyangs bstan p'ai nyi ma, an abbot of the Ngor school and the present head of Matho monastery. He arrived Matho monastery in 1968 at the request of his holiness Sakya Trizin, head of Sakya tradition. It is very unfortunate for the Matho monastery and the followers of Sakya tradition in Ladakh that due to the lack of leadership over many years Matho monastery had degenerated greatly, as a result the monastic activities of Matho and its sister concern could not flourish very well in Ladakh and its neighboring regions such as Lahaul and Spiti etc. However, under the leadership of klu lding mkhan rinpoche the religious affairs of the monastery had been on a firm and steady increase. Rinpoche began new programmes at the monastery. He revived old traditions which were in danger of being lost and greatly inspired monks and layman alike to practice Sakya tradition. He had bestowed monk's ordination upon many people and given Dharma teachings all desirous of religions. In addition he practised many meditation retreats in recent years as well as instigating share to do the same. He had been concentrated his much time in the renovation of the assembly hall and its decoration with religious objects and wall painting as Buddha as well as one hundred smaller ones all of which have gold overleaf and preserved in New dukhang and sometimes called Jamyang Lhakhang. Besides many smaller ones. In these and many other ways Rinpoche had sought the upliftment of the monastery and diligently worked for the monastic administration as well as for its activities.

4

Matho Cultural Welfare Society and Administration

In 1968 Skyabje Luding khan rinpoche visited Ladakh. He stayed in Matho monastery for 10 years up to 1978. During this period he gave preachings to laymen, Lamas and others. For Lamas he gave preachings on gechul gi dompa (Tib. dge-tsul slong gi sdom pa) and Gelong gidompa. In 1978 Luding khan Rinpoche founded mantho varler Norpa (Tib. Man tu va yer nor ma) gonpa. Therefore, he had to go and could not live long in Ladakh, probably in the same period Lama Sarchok (Tib. dge gsar mchog) strengthened the Sakya tradition. Gradually to lookafter the cash and kind property of the monastery, Matho Cultural Welfare Society came into existance.[1] To assist the Gonpa Welfare Society, the monastic administration was also made effective. Today to lookafter the gonpa administration lamas of the monastery work at different posts according to their seniority. Here follows the details.[2]

Lopon (Tib, slob dpon)

↓

Umzat (Tib. dbu mdzad)

↓

Nerpa (Tib. Gnyer pa)

↓

Komner (Tib. Dkor gnyer che chung)

↓

Chotpon (Tib. Mchod-dpon)

↓

Chotyog (Tib. Mchod gyod For the period 1-2 ys)

↓

Tung-pa (Tib dung pa) [For the period 1 to 2 ys]

↓

Gyaling pa (Tib. rgya-gling pa)[For the period 1 to 2 ys]

↓

Cook (Tib. ma byan pa) [For the period 1 to 2 years]

As layman offer his child to the monastery, he has to learn some primary Buddhist text under the guidance of senior Lama. On every big ceremony at the monastery he has to work with senior Lama and known 'ma-yan-pa; gradually he is promoted as Gyaling pa, and play Gyaling musical instrument during prayers. After working at the post of tung pa for two years he has to work as Chotyog. This time his duty is to make chotpa' or other related objects from 'Sattu'. Thereafter as Chotpon' he work as a senior partner of Chotyog and is responsible to arrange all necessary things as required during every important prayers. Then he is promoted as komner' (or Pujari), this time his duty is to worship daily at the concern temple. In the monastery he is first appointed as junior 'komner' then to senior 'komner'. Thereafter he is promoted as 'Umzat'. At this post he is responsible to start prayer. The other monks according to his directions read concern pothis and offer prayer. Finally he becomes Lopon (Tib. slob- dpon) or Deputy head Lama of the monastery. Besides, according to seniority he may become Chagzot who always accompany the head Lama and works as his private secretary.

In order to keep faith on Sakya tradition, time to time top ranking Lamas are invited to Matho monastery for preaching. On 26th June 1999 skyabgon Dag chen Dorje chang (Tib. skyabs mgon bdag chen rdo-rje' chang) visited Ladakh, he gave preaching to laymen for 26 days at the ground near the monastery. Besides he gave valuable suggestions to Lamas and the members of the Cultural Welfare Society Mangtro Gonpa, i.e, how to preserve the ancient old Sakya Buddhist tradition in the monastery as well work for the welfare of human beings.[3]

In olden days like other big monasteries, Lamas from Ladakh used to go to Tibet for higher studies.

The Lamas from Matho monastery were also deputed to Sakya monasteries in Tibet for higher studies, normally they studied there for three years. After returning in Ladakh they worked at the monastery in various responsible posts turn by turn. Sometimes Matho Lamas did not return to Matho gonpa. They worked in the concerned monasteries in Tibet. This tradition was stopped in 1959 after the occupation of Tibet by China. However to preserve this tradition, in 1989 a gonpa school Tsechhen was opened at Matho monastery. This school was later taken over by Central Institute of Buddhist Studies, Leh-Ladakh.[4] Today it has more than thirty students (novices). They are taught upto primary standard. The Central Institute of Buddhist Studies depute one teacher, who teaches them Bodhi, Hindi, English, Maths etc. All the novices are given stipend from the Central Institute of Buddhist Studies. The novices after completing their education at this Gonpa school, come to Central Institute of Buddhist Studies Leh for further studies. But most of them go to Muandgod, Dheradun and Mussoori; and study there in Sakya Colleges run by Tibetan exile monks.

At present Matho monastery has about 120 registered Lamas, 60 of them stay in the monastery, the rest are studing in the different institutions viz. Mundgod (Karnataka), Sampurnanand Sanskrit University (Varanasi), Tibetan Higher studies (Sarnath), Dehradun (Uttarakhand), Mussoori (Uttarakhand) Himachal Pradesh and Central Institute of Buddhist Studies, Choglamsar, Leh-Ladakh.

NOTES AND REFERENCES

1. Jamyang Gyaltsan (ed.): *Mangtro Monastery,* Cultural and Welfare Society, Mangtro Monastery, Leh, 2005.
2. *Ibid.,* p. 60.
3. *Ibid.,* p. 56.
4. Central Institute of Buddhist Studies, Leh-Ladakh. It was established in 1959. In 1972, it was given financial support by the Department of Culture. Govt. of India.

5

History of Matho Monastery

It is remarkable to note that originally the actual name of Matho monastery is Mangtro, which in Tibetan language is popularly known Thubten shaling chokar (or Thubstan chosling). Later the same corrupted to the present name in the following way:

Mangtro	≥	Mang stro
Mang stro	≥	Man tro
Man tro	≥	Mang tho
Mangtho	≥	Matho

In 1268 A.D. chos-rgyal Phagspa wanted to spread Sakya order[1] throughout it in Tibet. The same later was propagated by the learned Lamas in Tibet excluding Maryul (Ladakh). In those days Ladakh region was known as Maryul. Subsequently in 1415 Tungpa Dorje Palzang, a Sakya school's Lama, visited Ladakh. He was a Siddha Lama and had the capacity to control lhas and lhamas or evil spirits. When he came in Ladakh, two lhas also followed him. They were very strong and violent. Thereafter to propitiate them Tungpa Dorje Palzang made sacrificial cakes. But lhas did not want to go lower Valley of Indus. Thus, to settle them in the upper part of the Valley, Dorje Palzang came to Matho, made Lha-to for them near the Khar.

The two lhas (or protectors) were brothers, lived at kawa karpo in Khan the eastern part of Tibet. Having became local deities of that area they attached to the Tungpa Dorje Palzang, later popularly known as Nangrang. Today there are seven lhas of this cult in Ladakh, called seven brothers (Table 5.1)

TABLE 5.1

Seven Lha Brothers in Ladakh

Sl. No.	Name of Lha	Number	Village
1.	Nangrang	02	Matho
2.	Cakrang	02	Gya
3.	Skarang	02	Stok
4.	Jagnam	01	Skrubuchan

Note: According to local people there is only one Lha at Gya and other is in Thiksey.

After sometimes Tungpa Dorje came to Matho for making Lhato for Lhas. Later went to Zurkhang khar.

He stayed in Chotkhang of this khar, meditated for sometime and decorated one side wall by a beautiful fresco of Dandi Mahakala.[2] It is said that while making the fresco he did not find red stone colour, therefore used blood from his nose.

This was the period when Dragspa Bumde[3] was the king of Ladakh. He was planning to build Tesru Chorten[4] for the welfare of his citizens. Tungpa Dorje in those day got popularity as scholar Lama throughout the Ladakh. King invited him for the *rabnas*[5] of Tesru Chorten, accordingly went king's palace, "His Majesty did you call me".

"Yes Gyan le. In my kingdom people work hard, cultivate their land, but unfortunately do not get the yield as they expected. I feel there is something wrong. May be some evil spirits do not want to see my kingdoms progress and my citizens live peacefully without suffering. I do not want my citizens should live in unhealthy atmosphere. So for their welfare I have decided to build Tisru chorten. I hope by doing so evil spirits may stop their nonsense activities and my people may live peacefully. You are a good Buddhist scholar, can understand my feelings. I request you to perform *rabnas* for the said chorten."

"Your Highness I understand your feelings. I have no problems and will perform *rabnas.*"

Near Leh, rabnas was performed under the direction of Lama Tungpa Dorje palzang for Tesru Chorten. On this occasion Lamas of all sects took part in large number alongwith people of the country. After the successful completion of the *rabnas* ceremony, king became happy, he once again invited Tungpa Dorje at his palace.

"Your Majesty : Julley, I am here at your service."

"Gyan le. I am happy for your works, under your guideline *rabnas* is completed peacefully without any interruption. I feel happy if you please construct a monastery of your sect in Ladakh. I offer you Matho, Stakna, Shey and Marshelang villages for this auspicious work. You may build your monastery anywhere in Ladakh according to your wish."

"Thank you very much your highness."

Thereafter in search of proper place for Sakya monastery he visited many villages including Stakna, Shey and Marshelang. When he arrived Matho, stayed once again in Zurkhang. At Matho he felt lhas liked the place and did not want to leave Matho hillock. Thus, retreated for sometime at Chotkhang in Zurkhang. Subsequently climbed the Matho cave for meditation. He did not feel comfortable and experienced that the hillock would be harmful for Indus valley as well for Leh town. He came out from the cave and cut a portion of the unauspicious hillock, performed retuals and purified the whole hillock, later he constructed a chorten 'Riu Tashi Od tho'. After the construction of this chorten king Dragspa Bumde also felt that something happened good in his kingdom.

After the completion of 'Riu Tashi Od Tho' chorten, Tungpa Dorje palzang once again retreated in Matho cave. This time he felt comfortable and was able to finish meditation properly. When he came out from meditation cave, saw two deer were sitting peacefully without fear as if they were also doing meditation. Tungpa Dorje thought deer would be an auspicious sign for his Sakya tradition. Therefore decided that he should build his monastery on the hillock of Matho village. He informed king Drugspa Bumde about this decision. To know Tungpa Dorje palzang's decision king became very happy. He readily came forward and again called him at his palace.

"Your Majesty, as you know I have decided to build a Sakya monastery in Matho hillock. The hillock is not good for

Ladakh kingdom. Therefore, to ouster the bad shadow upon kingdom a Sakya monastery on the hillock is essential. I hope you will agree with my decision."

"I agree with your decision, when I came to know that you are going to build a Sakya monastery in Matho village, I felt as if my kingdom would progress culturally and economically. I know the establishment of any religious institution need administrative and public support. Therefore, to fulfil such demands I donate you lands from Chemdly, Marshelang, stagna, Stok, Rumtse and Cumathang in order to support your monastic activities. You may have sufficient Lamas from these villages."

About the land allotment for the Matho monastery, Dr. Jamyang Gyaltsan has the following opinion:

> "One morning at sunrise a deer was seen lying on a stone at the site of the present (Matho) monastery. This was connected with the deer park at Varanasi where Buddha preached his first sermon and this was inferred as a good omen to build the monastery. Thereafter, the monastery was named Tubtan Sha-ling choskor. The monk (Tungpa Dorje) then asked more land and as additional grant was made at Chamre, Sakti, Marshelang, Stakna, Stok, Gya, Rumtse, Chumathang, Kesar, Tiri, Skidmang and the Spiti, 70 houses were also attached for the upkeep of the monastery" Cf. Jamyang Gyaltsan: 'Mangtro Monastery,' Cultural Welfare Society, Mangtro Gonpa; 2005:18.

Thus by the kind support of king Dragspa Bumde, Tungpa Dorje palzang founded Gon-khang in 15th century A.D. Gradually after the establishment of Gon-khang temple in Matho monastery people from Ladakh started to offer their children to Monastery for religious works as Lamas. The Lamas thereafter got monastic education under the Sakya tradition. Many of them became famous throughout in Ladakh. Here are listed a few prominent Lamas among them.

1. Sonam Lados
2. Dungpa Sodsras khanchen
3. Lodos Gyatso
4. Dungpa khanpo
5. Dungpa Shesrabs Legspa

6. Dungpa Gyatso
7. Dungpa Gyaltsan.

With the passage of time Matho monastery became famous Buddhist centre in Ladakh. It thus required to build more temples and following temples were gradually built.

1. Gon-khang (1440)
2. Lhundup Lhakhang (During king Tsewang Namgyal)
3. Dukhang Ningpa (During 15th Century)
4. Dukhang Soma or Janyang Lhakhang (1970 and renovated again in 2007)
5. Dolma Lhakhang (During 1970).

The Gon-khang and Dukhang Ningpa were built during Tungpa Dorje Palzang period. However, after the parinirvana of Tungpa Dorje some other learned Lamas of this monastery viz Sonam Lodo Dung pa gyatso, Lodos gyatso etc., gave their firm support in making Buddhist images, publishing religious *pothis* and other related works. Many of these learned monks became head of the monastery and thoroughly increased its activities like other big monasteries in Ladakh viz. Thiksey,[6] Phyang,[7] Likir,[8] Spituk,[9] Hemis[10] and Lamayurul.[11] Matho monastery also started to send Lamas to sakya and Ngor in Tibet for higher studies in Buddhist philosophy, Buddhist Literature etc, under Sakya tradition. After completing education in Tibet they returned to Ladakh and started to perform ritual ceremonies and practise meditation according to the above two religious centres. In this way rituals and prayers are conducted at the monastery today have been preserved an unbroken link with the old religious tradition as practised in Tibet.

Sakya tradition in Ladakh flourished very well till king Jamyang Namgyal. When Balti war broke out, king Janyang Nangyal recruited Lamas from Matho in order to protect Ladakh from enemy. Unfortunately king Jamyang lost the battle and was taken Skardu as prisoner. Baltis reached upto Leh, they destroyed many monasteries on way and taken precious status to skardu. Matho monastery was also destroyed by them. Balti army, thus damaged Matho monastery buildings as much as they could. It was great loss as in the monastery there was neither Lamas nor proper temples existed, no one left in the monastery who could lookafter monastery property. Thereafter villages of Matho came forward, with the help of a few Lamas they built a Chorten on the decease head Lama (may be kunga Gyaltsan) of Matho. In the meanwhile this sad news spread in Tibet. To witness on spot situation Lama choskyi Lotos came in Ladakh. The situation of monastery buildings was so bad that he could not make any decision and was waiting king Jamyang Namgyal. After sometime king was released by Balti king. He came to Ladakh and regained the throne of Ladakh kingdom, later Lama choskyi Lotos met him.[12]

"Your Majestey, I came here to inform you about the pity condition of Matho monastery. In the monastery there is no Lama. All the important buildings are being destroyed by Baltis. They need huge repairing works. Now I request your Highness to visit the monastery and do something needful, so that the existence of Sakya order may not be completely washed away."

"I have listened you carefully, I will company you to Matho and inform you about my decision."

To acknowledge the devastating condition of Matho monastery king Jamyang Namgyal discussed the matter with their Ministries, he decided to repair the monastery buildings. By the end of 16th Century maximum temples in the monastery were repaired. Soonafter Lama Kungga Paldan visited Matho. He also gave his precious time in the repairing and rebuilding temples. Lama Lotos brought kangyur pothi from Tibet for the monastery thereafter konchok Tanzin, Lama Thinles kabab, Lama Lhundup chosphel, Lama Sakya Jangpo, Lama Thinle Phunchok, Lama Kunga Jangpo, Lama Thinle Phunchok, Lama Kunga, Cundus etc, made their wholehearted support for strengthening the Sakya order in Ladakh.

After the death of Jamyang Namgyal his son Singge Namgyal became the king of Ladakh. He supported Drug pa ka'gyud tradition. Thus the lands which were earlier under Matho monastery given to Hemis monastery. During Singge Namgyal regime Matho did not get good support from King's administration. Consequently, the influence of Sakya tradition in Ladakh gradually decreased in the villages, where it had good number of Sakya families, did not offer their children to monastery as novices. Thus the strength of Lamas in the monastery also started decreasing.

During 18th Century differences between king Phunchok Nangyal and Vassale king of Parig Khuvo Tashi Namgyal took place. Later it became so acute that there was possibility of war. This news came in Tibet. His Holiness Dalai Lama when came to know about this incident, decided to remove the differences between them and avoid the possibility of war in Ladakh. Tsewang Norbu went to Ladakh and resolved the above problems amicably. In 1753 he arrived in Ladakh. In order to solve the problems called series of meetings of all ranked officials from both sides. Finally he was successful in avoiding the impending war in Ladakh, later he dedicated himself in the propagation of Buddhism. This time Matho monastery had only a few Lamas. Therefore, to strengthen Sakya tradition, Matho gonpa authority decided to invite Kathok Rigzin Tsewang Narbu. Then *Lhun dup khang* walls were decorated by beautiful frescos. Kunjong Khorlo observed that in those days Kathok Rigzin Tsewang was a good scholar, he promoted painting works in Ladakh.

In 1926 Langdrag Khanchep Chamba Nankha Kungzang tanve gyaltsen of Ngor visited Ladakh. He stayed in Matho monastery. His presence in the monastery helped to strengthen the Lama tradition. Thereafter Lama Jalu Thinchen Jecun Nawang Khenab also stayed in monastery however, did not stay more. Consequently, Matho monastery faced the problem of head Lama, who could lookafter the activities of Sakya tradition and help to promote this tradition throughout in Ladakh. Keeping in view the above facts, Lamas of the monastery went to Tansung and Rongtsan Tandol oracals. They requested "In the interest of Sakya order Matho monastery need head Lama. Therefore kindly tell them a amiable path."

Oracle replied : "If Matho people and Lamas of the monastery together will go to north India in Mussoorie, Uttarakhand and request the head of Sakya order His Holiness Sakya Thizin Dolma Padong Nawang Kanga Thekcen Sparbar Thinlas Vang gi Gyalpo to depute a head Lama to Matho monastery, your problem may be solved."

Later a Buddhist delegation went to Mussorie and met the head of Sakya sect. They requested to depute a head Lama for Matho monastery in order to look after the monastery function properly. The head Lama of Sakya order accepted their request and deputed Luding Khan rinpoche as head of Matho monastery. In 1968 he arrived in Ladakh. He was given warm welcome under the leadership of K.G. Bakula[12] of Ladakh Buddhist Association and Representative of Gonpa Association.

Thereafter on the request of His Holiness Sakya Trizin, head of the Sakya sect Luding Khan Rinpoche stayed in Ladakh for 16 days. He passed instructions to the Matho gonpa authorities and asked them to look after Gonpa property carefully. In 1999, once again he visited Ladakh and gave preachings on various aspects of Buddhism. This time he paid his attention to strengthen Sakya order in Ladakh and asked Matho Gonpa Welfare Society to look into this matter seriously if possible to do needful action. Today the monastery is functioning under the direction of Matho Gonpa Welfare Society. Notably, in July 2007 renovation works started in monastery in order to preserve the old Jamyang structure and remove the damaged part of the temple by centered pillars, so that further damages and cracks would be prevented further. Thus, the whole monastery structure of the Matho hillock can be protected.

NOTES & REFERENCES

1. Sakya Order: Tib Sa-skya (Pron. Sakya). The name of this Mahayana Tradition of Buddhism is derived from the main Sakya (or Sa-skya) monastery situated at the bank of Grum River 94 km southwest of Xigaze. Cf. Finegan Jack, *Tibet: A Dreamet of Image*. Tibet House, New Delhi, 1986, 88.
2. Dandi Mahakala: Tib. equivalent mgon-po-beng. A Dharmapala. He is identified by one face, fierce three eyes, two hands carrier dorje in his right and skull up in left. A stick rests on his hands across his body. Cf. Bunce, Fredric W.: *An Encyclopedia of Buddhist Deities, Demigods, Godlings, Saints and Demons*, Vol. I D.K. Print World, New Delhi, 1994, 114.

3. *Dragspa Bumde:* A renowned Lha Chen dragspa bun lde, popularly called Lde. He was the eldest and ought to have been king alone. By nature he was thoughtful about even the low-caste people among his subjects, mild and merciful disposition and was inclined towards Buddhism. He erected many religious buildings. In Namgyal Tsemo Hill temple made a wood and clay statue of Maitreya in a sitting posture. His earnest desire was to purify Buddhism of his country. Cf. Francke A.H., *A History of Western Tibet,* Reprint Asian Educational Services, New Delhi; New Delhi 1995, pp. 75-78.
4. *Tesru Chorten:* (Pron Tisorru). The name of this Chorten is derived from the Tibetan word Tesu-gser-po (i.e. mule shaped yellow rock). In olden days a evil spirit lived in the cavity of Tesru which was very harmful causing disaster, sickness and other calamities in the Leh valley. In order to get rid of them, king Bumde (Bumlde) with the advice of Lamas erected the above chorten. It had 108 Chapels.
5. *Rabnas:* (Consecrate): Dragspa Bumde called Tungpa Dorje to Consecrate the newly constructed Tesru chorten.
6. *Thiksey:* Thiksey monastery is 19 km from Leh spectacularly sited. It is one of the largest and architecturally most impressive gonpas. There are several temples in this gonpa containing images, stapes and well paintings.
7. *Phyang:* 17 km from Leh on the Leh-Kargil road, it looks like a huge palace from far distance founded by Tashi Nangyal in the later half of the 16th Century A.D.
8. *Likir:* This monastery was founded in 11th Century A.D. Later in 18th Century re-founded under Geluk Pa order.
9. *Spituk:* It is situated 8 km from Leh. This monastery belongs to Geluk–Pa Tradition and situated on the top of a hillock in Spituk village.
10. *Hemis:* 40 km from Leh. This monastery is one of the biggest gonpa of Drugpa tradition. It was built during King Singge Namgyal in 1630 A.D. Hemi Tesru is the famous festival of this monastery.
11. During the period of great fighting between the Baltis and Ladakhis Matho monastery was almost destroyed. King Jamyang Namgyal was imprisoned. The head Lama of the Matho monastery was also killed in this war. However. king later released. Choskyi Lotos, who took the charge of the monastery then met him. King pleased with him and returned all his lands to the monastery.

Besides he bestowed more land. Lama Choskyi Lotos renovated the monastery and restore monastic activities with the kind help of king Jamyang Namgyal. He was 23rd king in the sequence from Pelgyigon.

12. *Rev. K.G. Bakula:* He was head Lama of Spituk monastery then the president of Ladakh Gonpa Association.

6

Cultural Monuments in Matho

1. Go-nga Chorten[1]

In simple way we call it five heads chorten. In Matho such chortens are built surrounding the monastery each at the north, south, east, and west directions. According to Buddhist tantra (Tib. rgyal), there are four types of tantra:

1. Cha gyud
2. Chot gyud
3. Nalzor gyud
4. Naljor Lamet gyut.

Lotsava Rinchen Zangpo,[2] the great scholar and translator during 10-11th Century A.D. had practiced Naljor Lamet gyut. It is said that the five headed chorten is the symbol of Naljor Lamet gyut Buddhist tantra, It is an auspicious monument of Mahayana Buddhism, which helps to preserve Buddhist tradition and strengthen monastic system for the benefit of all human beings.

Rongtsan Karmar (Tib. Rong-btsan-dkar-dmer) Lhato

It is situated about 7-8 km from the Matho village in Rong. One can see good vegetation and feel peaceful environment, free from all types of pollution. At the end of Matho Nangrang the oracles get up early in the morning, take bath, perform morning prayer etc, and leave the monastery. At a certain place along the way to the original shrine (Lhato)[3] they enter into trance and ride on horse until they reach the Rongtsan Karmar Lhato. It is made of juniper shrubs. Here they examine the grains which are contained in a vase that is in the shrine itself.

Finally the protectors leave the bodies of the oracles and absorb into the Lhato which has been recently exchanged by fresh juniper. This place is ritually pure free from evil spirits as it is a seat of Rong-btsan-dkar-dmar deities who help people to achieve happiness and remove the obstacles on the path of Buddhahood. Thus ultimately they ensure that no harm comes to the Buddha Dharma.

Ci pur chan phug (Tib. Ci pur Tsan Phug) Cave

This Cave is situated about 8-9 km from Matho village in the upper part of the valley. It is naturally made by huge boulder. Fresh water flows through nearby. Since olden days, Yogis retreated and sometimes flew in sky.

Dorje Tag

It is about 6-7 km from Matho village, situated in the upper side of the valley. Here people and Tibetan doctor come for chu-tsan (medicinal water). The water which flows here is used for the treatment of eye and stomatch diseases.

Rangjon (Naturally Made Images): There are many naturally made images on the rocks nearby Dorje Tag such as :

1. Dolma[4]
2. Kesar's arm[5]
3. Hoof print of Kesar's horse
4. Saddle print of Kesar's horse.

Tse Tsau Cave: This meditation cave is near Matho monastery in upper side of the valley. In olden day Gotsang pa, a great Buddhist Yogi, came here for meditation. Once Gotsangpa[6] visited Matho village for begging. He came to an old lady had only door and asked to donate something. The lady had only a piece of sheep flesh, which she gave it to Gotsangpa. In evening her husband returned. He asked for flesh. The lady said:

> "I did not have anything to give to Gotsangpa. Therefore I gave that flesh to him."

The old man became angry on her. He abused his wife as well as Gotsangpa. Next day Gotsangpa flew to the high mountain towards his monastery and stop at the cave about to the mountain near Hemis. Through his spiritual power he threw a bowl on one side of cave rock. The bowl print emerged on the rock. Then Gotsangpa forecasted "Yesterday evening at Matho village an old man absused me for a piece of flesh. Now the print of bowl will show the destiny of his family. Till we see bowl print on the rock, the family will not improve the living standard."

It is said according to the Gotsangpa prediction the concern family economic standard is not very good.

Sri Devi Natural Cave: Sri Devi cave is about 2 km above the Matho cave (Tib. Tse Tsa Cave). In this cave pilgrims can not enter with heavy woollen cloths. They have to put off heavy clothing if they want to go inside the cave for prayer. Here Paldan Lhamo[7] natural image is made on one side of rock. The image of Paldan Lhamo is clearly visible but the mule upon which she rides and the five retines which surround her are not clear.

Dorje Palzang Temple: In 15th Century A.D. Tung pa Dorje Palzang[8] visited Matho village, stayed in a cave below the Matho monastery. Here he made a small temple for his meditation and stupa by storchu.[9]

In nutshell there are many sites of cultural heritage at Matho which have religious importance, need conservation in order to keep intact the cultural tradition.

NOTES & REFERENCES

1. Go-nga Chorten (Tib. ngo-lnga chorten): They are eight in Matho four at the surrounding of Matho monastery and rest in the other parts of village. In olden days under Lama tradition, like other monasteries in Ladakh Lamas from the Matho used to go to Tibet to listen Lamdas ka-wang. They were exempted from any kind of offerings to attend the above function. The head Lama of Norpa sect decided to change the past tradition, and asked Ladakhis to donate something. The Tibetan administration when came to know about that decision, immediately asked head Lama to resume the older tradition. Thereafter the Lamas of Matho monastery unanimously decided to build Go-nga chortens in response to peaceful solution of above decision.
2. Lotsana Rinchen Zangpo : He was born in a Kyuvang Darni village, in Guge district of western Tibet, in 958 A.D. His father

gzhonu dbang phyag and mother kun-bzang shesrab brtan wanted his son should be a scholar Lama. So they sent his son to Kashmir for higher education on Buddhism. He went Kashmir three times and received teaching on Buddhism from 75 teachers.

3. ***Lhato:*** It is a symbol of Lha's shrine. Usually we may see Lhatos in every village on the top of hillocks, on the top of high passes and on the roof of the main phaspun's house. In Tibetan 'Pha' means father and 'Spun' to relation. According to Ladakhi Buddhist custom under Magpa marriage system Lha will be the same of father side. In reverse when boy or girl leaves parental house, the Lha of the newly married family will base upon where they stay.
4. ***Dolma:*** In Sanskrit she is equivalent to Tara. She is a female tutelary deity with various forms, who is regarded as the manifestation of Avaḷokitesvara. The following five Taras are common in Ladakh : 1. White Tara, (2) Green Tara (3) Blue Tara (4) Red Tara and (5) Yellow Tara.
5. ***Kesar's Arm:*** Kesar was a powerful king in olden days. In Ladakh some scholars believe he was the incarnation of Avalokitesvara. His arm's carving can be seen on the rock.
6. ***Gotsangpa:*** In Tibetan language equivalent rgod-tsang-Pa-mgon-po-dpal. He was born in 1189. Later he became the disciple of gtzang-pa-rgyas-ras, and was treated as the main disciple. It is said that before coming to the selter of gtzang-pa; four wandering minstrels happened to come to his native village, singing some verses like. "The chos-rje rgya-ras of rva-lung holds a fruit, bestowing bliss for the present life and for practising the holy Dharma, should go to Rva-lung, a dedicated and determined person must go to him." To listen these verses God-tsang-Pa decided to leave his home and study under the guidance of gtzang-Pa-rgyas-ras. Later he studied under his teacher and practise meditation. Cf. Nawang Tsering. *Buddhism in Ladakh;* Sterling Publishers Pvt. Ltd., New Delhi, 1979: 25.
7. Paldan Lhamo : "Tib. dpal ldan lha mo; Sridevi," glorious goddess, is apparently a form of the Hindu devi Kali, Durga, Parvati. She is one of the most important protectors of Geluk Pa (Tib. Gelugs pa) tradition of Buddhism and the guardian of Lhasa. She is a consort of Yama, shown seated sideways on her horse or mule. Cf. Finegan, Jack: *Tibet: A Dreamt of Image*, Tibet House, New Delhi, 1986 : 133.
8. Tung pa ***Dorje Palzang:*** He was a great Sakya scholar, visited

Ladakh in 1415 and established a temple in Matho village. The same was later developed as Matho monastery, the only Sakya monastery in Ladakh region. It is also known as 'Thup-bstan-sha-gling chos- khor' in Bhoti language. On residing in a cave located at the present site of the monastery he visited Dragspa Bumde, the king of Ladakh. In those days near Leh town a evil spirit was annoying the people of his kingdom. To know the ability of Dorje palzang, he called him to consecrate the newly constructed Tesru chorten at Leh. The evil spirit was also living there. After the construction of the said chorten and subsequently consecrated by Dorje Palzang, the activities of the evil spirit was stopped. King pleased with this he bestowed upon him a large tract of land extending from Tagna upto the Matho village.

9. Jamyang Gyaltsan: 'Mangtro monastery,' Cultural and Welfare Society, Mangtro Gonpa, Leh; 2005: 37.

7

Matho Oracles

In olden days tribes who settled down along the Indus banks worshipped natural things like; sun, moon, trees, mountains, water, earth, etc. They believed that these natural things have some spiritual powers. If they become angry something would go wrong. When Bon-religion[1] flourished by this, as a result Ladakhis strated to believe on Lha and Lhu (Tib. klu). Lha or gods in the sky are considered minor deities. They are honoured by special altars Lhato.[2] Lhus live in water. They are the deities of water and human world. In general 'lha' and 'lhu' are socially organised with the human world.

In 8th Century A.D. king Thrisong Desan (Tib khri strong lde-brtsan)[3] invited Padmasambhava[4] to cease the activities of Bonpos. Guru Padmasambhava visited Tibet. To understand the practical position he decided to establish Samye monastery. Construction work started. During day Padmasumbhva's men constructed the monastery, while in night spirits under the direction of Bonpo destroyed the same. This war continued for several days. Padmasambhava then placed statues of Bonpo deities alongwith Buddha. In this way Buddhism spread in Tibet . Thereafter the same during 10th century and onwards propogated in Ladakh. Like Tibet many Lhas also spread their roots up to Ladakh. At the passage of time Ladakhis believe them and according to Budhist tradition they started to pay their regards. The Matho Lhas also came from Tibet alongwith Lama Tungpa Dorje Palzang,[5] during 15th Century A.D. It is said that Rongstan Karmar (Tib. Rong- btsan dkar-dmar)[6] originally belong to Tibet. They were two brothers who lived in Kawa Karp, Kham region of eastern Tibet. As Lama Tungpa Dorje belongs to Kham regions. The Rongtsan Karmar were treated as local deities of the area and hence attached to Dorje Palzang. When he came to Ladakh the deities also followed him. Both deities were very powerful and violent and preferred to settle down in the upper part of Indus valley in the Matho area.

Every year from the 7th day to the 15th day of the first Tibetan month Lord Buddha's Miracle Day is celebrated first for seven days. Lamas of the monastery perform *Hevajra rituals.* On fourteenth and fifteenth *Mahakal puja* and cham tantric dance are performed. This time *Rongtsen Karmr* oracle activities bring special attention. Both the lhas run over the roofs of monastery and do miracles. On this occasion each individual try to ask about his/her future.[7]

Now a question may arise, how oracles are selected who act as Rangtsan kramar? The two Lamas are selected from the Lamas of they monastery. After performing certain meditation or ritual practice act as lhas, during Matho Nangrang perform miracle activities. Here follows the years on 15th of the 10th Tibetan month two Lamas from the Matho monastery are chosen according to seniority. They later act as oracles. The final selection of Lamas are done under a certain tradition. All the names of senior Lamas are put in a bowl which is slowly whirled around until two names fall out. In case after three attempts one Lama's name does not fall out he is never chosen as oracle. During the selection process, Lamas perform *Mahakala puja.* Those who are chosen as oracles must go through proper training, and have to go one year meditation. In the middle of meditation they propitiate Shri Hevajra, perform sacrificial cake offerings to the Dharma protectors and other activities. They remain in strict retreat during this period. i.e. from the Sakya Pandita's Mahaparinirvana Day on the fourteenth day of the eleventh month of the Tibetan calender until the sixth day of the first month meditate Hevajra, offer *tormas* (sacrificial cakes) to the Dharma protectors in general and especially to Rongtsan Karmar. Oracles training is not an easy task for Lamas, while retreating in a Matho cave they have to maintain neat and clean atmosphere, wear washed cloths, keep themselves clean bath once in a week with scented water. Each year they conclude their meditation on the tenth day of the Ist month. At the end Rongtsan Karmar (Tib. Rong btsan dkar-dmar) deities enter into their bodies. They immediately go into the trance. In this state they first visit monastery temple, followed by the Mahakala Shrine or Gonkhang, people are then allowed to ask questions. They answer them, go to another Mahakala shrine, called Chisa, sit on the balcony in front of shrine. Public in general are then allowed to meet them. On this occasion they predict events of the following year. They chose four men from the crowd to bring seven huge piles of juniper shrubs from Hemi shapachen or Skrubucan village situated in the lower part of Ladakh region. They remake their shrine the four main are given blessing and protective cords are bestowed and then they sent off. Next day, on 11th they again go into trance in their rooms. At this state they leave their room, go to the temple and Mahakala shrines then received high Lamas and officials. The oracles give presents their old cloths and other articles who accept them as tailsmans. In exchange the oracles are given new clothing and articles.

On 12th and 13th, they again enter into trance. They meet visitors and make predictions in response to individual questions.

On 14th, they go into trance as before come to the courtyard and perform religious dance with other Lamas who are dressed as Mahakala and surrounding deities, as well as two deer. The Lama who dressed as Mahakala performs a rite in which the two oracles watch over and assist. During these four days from 11th to 14th, the oracles come out of their trance on the courtyard where they perform religious dances. On the following day the oracles bathe and then draw their wrathful faces on their chests and backs. They are clothed tiger skin skirts, and adored with ornaments of bone and many relic bracelets, which were given by Ladakhi queen many years ago. A cloth mask with a small opening at the nose and much hair at the top, are on their faces. In their hands they hold a small drum and a wooden stick called *gende.* By beating drum they call monks to come together. On this day Rongtsan Karmar enter into the men in the form of the transcendental knowledge of Mahakala. The Vajra Master then perform a special ceremony with Lamas of the monastery.

On completion of the above ceremony the two oracles enter the temple holding above their heads the upper robe of Dorje

Palzang (Tib. rdo-rje dpa-bzang). This is the symbol of ancient oracles religious performance in the monastery when they would fly into the temple by holding this robe aloft. In the temple they receive blessings from the Vajra Master then visit the inner part of the temple Mahakala shrine, the ancient king's palace shrine and the Mahakala shrine in the lower part of the temple, known as Kalon Gonkhang. While visiting the above places they meet people and give predictions in response to their questions. Returning to courtyard they take roasted barley flower and throw it in every direction, the amount which falls indicates which part of the country will have good or bad crops. Finally the oracles pray for the preservation and promotion of Buddha Dharma and for the prosperity of the country, the trance then ends.[9]

"In this way 10th onwards the oracles do their normal daily prayers, make offerings at the shrines, receive scented water from the Vajramaster. Under the influence of trance state they run fast along the edge of the outer walls of the courtyard and the monastery roof, without ever falling. Sometimes cut their mouth and hands with sharp knives and bleed heavily. The following day surprisingly no trace of scars or wounds can be seen on their bodies.[10]

"On 15th the oracles go about with blindfolds. They are able to see through the eyes of the wrathful deities drawn on their chests and backs. This tradition was begun when Ladakhi queen desired to test the power of oracles and asked them to walk without opening their eyes along the edge of monastery's roof."[11]

The seventh and final day on which the oracles go into trance is the 8th day of the 2nd Tibetan month. In olden days early in the morning servants and horses were arrived from Hemis monastery and king palace of Ladakh. During 19th Century A.D. when king was dethroned from Ladakh kingdom, and was residing at Stok village near Leh. The horses are taken into the *Tangra* from Hemis monastery and Stok village one or two days before the ceremony.[12]

On the 8th day of 2nd month the oracles, leave the Matho monastery. At a certain place along the way to the upper part of the valley they enter into trance. In this state they ride on horses until reach the original shrine of Rongtsan Karmar, made of juniper shrubs. They examine the grains contained is a vase inside the shrine. This again foretells whether or not the crops will be good in the following year. At the end the protectors leave the bodies of the oracles, and are absorbed into the recently changed juniper at Lhato.

In conclusion, I would say through the Matho Nagrang two deities solve the problems of individuals and predict the future of Ladakhi society. By performing religious dances they ensure to preserve Sakya tradition.

NOTES & REFERENCES

1. Bon religion : Prior to Buddhism in Tibet there was an indigenous form of religion called Bon religion, its adherents and priests are called Bon-po. Trashi Gyentsen had written a comprehensive book on Bon works commonly called Lek-shadzed. Cf. Finegen, Jack: *Tibet : A Dreamt of Image,* Tibet House; 1986; 20-21.
2. Lhato : It is a shrine for Lha (or protective deity), and is made of juniper shrubs (locally called shakpas).
3. Thrisong Desan (Tib. Khri strong lde-brtsan) he was the son of the king Trhide Dusten and was the successor of his father and became the thirty-eighth king of Tibet of the yarlung Dynasty. In Tibetan language he was pronounced as khri srong lde brtsan (or Trhisong Detsen). He was born in 742. His father was died in a violence in 755, as a result Tshrisong Detsen who was only 13 years old occupied the throne of Tibet. He began a region which according to Jetsun Trakpa Gyentsen and Phakpa Lodro Gyentsen, extended for forth-three years until his death at the age of fifty six, probably in 797, Cf. . Finegan, Jack: *Tibet: A Dreamt of Image;* op. cit.; 47.
4. Padmasambhava: Tib : Lopon Rinpoche or Guru Rinpoche, i.e., "Lotus born One", an Indian Tantric invited by king Thrisong Detsen in the eighth century A.D. He brought Buddhist Tantra in Tibet during that time and subdued the local deities and demons while constructing the first Samyas monastery in Tibet. He helped Santaraksita in his works on Buddhism in Tibet. During his period Buddhism was amazingly spread throughout the Tibet. Later he was recognised by Tibetans as the second Buddha. He is seated on a lotus blossom that rises from a lake, his right foot resting on a smaller lotus blossom. Face one body,

flesh clour; hands, Two, holds vajra in his right hand: left holds skull cup containing a vase of the nectar of immortality; Carries a tantric staff.

5. Lama Trung-pa-do-je Palzang (Tib. bla-ma-Drung-Pa-rdo-rje Palsang): He was a Sakya Lama who arrived in Ladakh during 15th century A.D. When Dragspa Bumde was the king of Ladakh. He established the Matho monastery which later named as Thup-bstan-sha-gling chos-khor.
6. Rongtsan Karmar (Tib. Rong-btsan dkar-dmar) : They are the special protectors of Matho monastery. They were recognised by the blessing of Guru Padmasambhava at a holy place situated in eastern Tibet called Rongchhen Khawa Karpo and was linked with the tantric deity Cakrasamvara. When Dorje Palzang arrived in Ladakh these deities also followed him.
7. Luding Khan Rinpoche, Jamyang Tenpai Nyima: Mongtro Monastery; 1968 & Jamyang Gyaltsen; *Monks of Mongtro Gompa, In Recent Research on Ladakh,* 4 & 5, Motilal Banarsidass Publisher Pvt. Ltd., Delhi, 1995, 55-59.
8. *Ibid.*
9. *Ibid.*
10. *Ibid.*
11. *Ibid.*
12. *Ibid.* The Tangra is situated just above the main road near Matho monastery. Before Matho Nagrang horses are kept here. On 8th of 2nd Tibetan month both Matho Lhas go to Rongtsan Karmar shrine called Lhato to change the juniper shrubs by new shrubs. The horses on 7th on the final day of the Nagrang are used by Lhas to go upto original shrine of Rongtsan Karmar. At this shrine they perform certain rituals then the bodies of oracles are absorbed into recently exchanged juniper shrubs.

8

Gon Khang

Gon Khang (Tib. Mgon-Khang) of the Matho monastery was built in 16th century A.D. It has some old statues of Dharmpalas. Here follows the details:

1. Vajra Pinjarnath[1] : Made of brass
2. Mahakala[2] Tib. Gonpo : Made of brass
   : Head Four
3. Sridevi[3] Tib. Paldan Lhamo : Made of brass
4. Rong-tsan Kar-Mar : Matho oracles
   : Made of clay
   : Only during festival days public is allowed to see.

Gon-Khang temple is a dark room. It has wall painting of Buddhist deities in old tradition. The details are furnished below:

1. Padmasambhava[4]
2. Ishey Tsogial[5]
3. Mandarava[6]
4. Kunga Nying-po[7] : Sakya scholar
5. Sonam Tsemo[8] : Sakya scholar
6. Trak-pa gyaltsan[9] : A great scholar of Sakya tradition
7. Chos-rgyal Phagspa[10] : A Sakya scholar
8. Kunggagyaltsan : A Sakya scholar.

In fact, Gonkhang temple of Matho monastery is generally not open for common public. It can be opened only during annual festival.

NOTES & REFERENCES

1. *Vajra Pingarnath:* Cf. Jamyang Gyaltsan: Mangtro Monastery, 2005, p. 36.
2. Mahakala : Gonkhang has four faced Mahakala. He is considered the chief protector of the Buddha Dharma Here follows some lineage about the four faced gonpa:

(i) Once Nyen Lotsawa Dharmadrag lived in India. He received the teaching of Dharma protector for seven years, later along with five merchant friends he came Tibet, on route to Tibet he saw dreadful dream in which he was captured by king's troops. In the morning he told dream to his companions, they said: "This shows the indication that some interruption may come on our way." To know this fact Nyen Lotsawa flung a ritual cake. Spontaneously there arose a dark violent storm which engulfed the king's troops and finally except a handful Indian Acharyas all were killed including the king. This was the example that how gonpa protect his friends. Later Khau Dharma Gyaltsen received instructions from Nyen Lotsava, thereafter during 1092-1158 Sachen kunga Nying Po followed the same instructions and became the protector of the Sakya heads that Nagarjuna was the spiritual father of Four Faced Gonpo at Nalanda University. As Sakya Panditas, were holders of Nalanda lineage, Gonpo is considered as the protector of Sakya school. Thus Gonpo of four heads the protector of Buddha Dharma and the holders of the doctrine is known Ludrub spiritual father and son. Cf. Ladrang Kalsang. The Guardian Deities of Tibet, Little Lhasa Pub., Dharmasala, 2000, p. 33.

3. Sridevi: In Tibetan equivalent to Paldan Lhamo, dpal ldan lha mo "The glorious Goddess" is one of the most important protector of Geluk pa order of Buddhism. History tells us Paldan Lhamo was the jewel protector, extremely aggressive and was the custodian of religious properties. she was initiated by Chagna Dorje and was given the name Dorje Naljorma. Later Padmasambhava bound her to follow the exhaustive instruction and come to Tibet with him. Cf. Batchelor Stephen. The Tibet Guide; Wisdom Pub. London, 1987: 423-24 & Ladrang Kalsang, *The Guardion Deities of Tibet; op cit.*, 2000 : pp. 17-31.
4. Padmasambhava: Tib, Lopon rinpoche or Guru Rinpoche. "Lotus Born One." An Indian tantric invited by king Trisong Detsan in the eighth Century A.D. He brought Buddhist tantra in Tibet

during the above period and subdued the local deities and demons while constructing the first Samyas monastery in Tibet. He helped Santaraksita in his work on Buddhism in Tibet. During his period Buddhism was flourished and therefore he was recognised by Tibetans as the second Buddha. Cf. Bachelor Sptephen *op. cit.*, p. 420.

5. Ishey Tsogial (or Eshy Tsogyal) : The consort of Padmasambhava and depicted on the left side of him.
6. Mandarava : The consort of Padmasambhava and depicted on the right of him.
7. Kunga Nying Po (Tib. kun dga' snying po—1092-1102) : He was also called Sa chen (sachen) and recognised as an authoritative expounder of Sakya-pa religious doctrine Cf. Finegan Jack, *Tibet: A Dreamt of Image:* Tibet House & Wiley Eastern Ltd. New Delhi, 1986; 89.
8. Sonam Tsemo: (Tib. bsod nams rtse mo) (1142-1182). He was the son of Kung Nying po and devoted himself in religious works. Thus helped to enhance the activities of Sakya tradition of Mahayana.
9. Trak-pa gyaltsan (or grags pa rgyal mtshan) (1147-1216). He was the son of Kung Nying po and devoted himself to religious activities.
10. Chos- rgyal phagspa : (Tib, Phags pa blo gros rgyal mtshan) (1235-1280). He is generally known as 'Phags pa. He devoted himself in religious works.

In the Gonkhang after a gap of one year I was allowed to see the wall paintings, which were very old of 16th century A.D. and was drawn by golden colours. Such paintings I also saw in old Lhamo Khang temple of Thiksey monastery in Ladakh. This time I saw the painting which I did not included earlier such as:

(1) Virupa (Tib. grup p'ai dbang phyug biru va pa): He was the Mahasiddha. and gave teaching on Hevajra tantras to Sakya scholars.

(2) Lam das lhagyud (Tib. lam abras-bla brgyud).

(3) Namsras terdag gyad (Tib. rnam sras-gter bdag brgyat).

(4) Dolzang (Tib. sgrol lzang btsas bzhuge yod tsing). In Sanskrit equivalent Green Tara.

9

Tse Chen Zims Chung

The Tse Chen Zims chung of Matho monastery is built for high ranked Lamas or rinpoches, H.H. Skyabje Luding Khan rinpoche used to stay in this room and sometimes meditated here. During winter seasons he stayed and meditated. This room has following status.

1. Ngor Chen Kunga Zangpo (Tib. ngor chen kun dg'a bzang po).[1]
2. Sakya Thub pa (Tib. ston pa sha'kya thub pa).[2]
3. Canrazig (Tib. Spyan ras gzigs).[3]

All the above status are made of Serzang (Tib, gser zangs). Besides, this Zims Chung has many thankas. Eleven of them are in good condition. Here follows a list of thankas.

1. Gongma namna (tib. gong rnam lng'ai)
2. Sakya Pandita[4]
3. Opakmed mandala (Tib. 'aod dpag med-kyi zhing bkar[5]
4. Dorje Zhunu (Tib. rdo rje gzhon nu)[6]
5. Tsogdag (Tib. tshogs bdag lha brgyad)[7]
6. Guru lha (Tib. guru lha brgyad)
7. Drubthob gya cu (Tib. grub thob brgyad cu)
8. Choskyong yul lha (Tib. chos skyong- yul lha)
9. Jamyang Sangyas (Tib. 'ajam dbyangs sangas rgyas dpal dpal bzang)
10. Jigjed (tib. 'ajigs byed)[8]
11. Dorje chang (Tib. rdo rje 'achang).[9]

NOTES & REFERENCES

1. Ngor Chen Kunga zangpo: He was great scholar of Sakya, founder of Ngor lineage, a branch of Sakya tradition, born in 1382 and got parinirvana in 1457.
2. Sakya Thub Pa: Buddha Sakyamuni (or Sakyamuni Buddha). Prince Siddhartha Gautama of Sakya, " The enlightened One. The historical Buddha who become defined and the prototype for other Buddhas. A Manushi Buddha of the present age. His Manushi Buddhashahti is Yasodhara and his Manushi Bhodisattva is Ananda. Also known as Gautama Buddha. Cf. Bunce, Fredrick W.: *An encyclopedia of Buddhist Deities, Demigods, Godlings Saints and Demons;* D.K. Printworld Pvt, New Delhi; Vol. I, 1994, pp. 469-70.
3. Canrazig; The compassionate one, he looks in every direction. A Mahabodhisattva and one of the most popular Buddhisattva in the world of Buddhism. He is the embodiment of compassion. The fourth Dhyani Buddhisattva the creator and ruler of the present age an emanation of Dhyani Buddha Amitabha who was born from a shining, white ray of light which sprang from this Dhyani Buddha's eye after a long and deep by the meditation. He is considered by the Northern Buddhists as one of the right Dhyani Buddhisttvas. Cf. Bunce, Fredric W. *op. cit.*, 35.
4. Sakya Pandita: He was the older son of Pelchen Opo, known kunga Gyaltsen (or kung Gyaltsen). He entered the religious life and eventually became the abbot of Sakya attaining such a reputation that he was simply known as Sakya Pandita (pron. Sakya scholar"). Cf. Finegan, Jack, *Tibet: A Dreamt of Image,* Tibet House, New Delhi, 1986, p. 105.
5. Opakmed: In Sanskrit equivalent Amitabha. A Dhyani Budha oriented in the west. His recognition symbol is the lotus (Padma). Water and the night are his associations. He is the lord of the heavenly Sakhavati (Dewa chen). The personification of the five Buddha energies and represents the lotus energy which changes passion into spiritual purity. He may be portrayed sitting on a peacock throne. Cf. Bunce, Fredrick. W. *op. cit.*, 11-12.
6. Dorje Zhunu: The Tibetan transliteral equivalent of the Sanskrit for Vajrakumara. One of the deities pictured in the Astasahasrika Pantheon. Face: three fierce, three eyes each, flame like hair. arms six principal hands embrace shakti in dharmachakra mudra and holding ritual dagger (phur-bu) right hands hold thunderbolts.

left hands hold karuna mudra and trident (trishula); mudra; dharmachakra and karana; body; Corpulent spread vajra- Hipped voings in yab-yam position legs–two; Asana–alidhasana; ornaments five skull crown wristlets, anklets necklace, garlands of freshly severed heads tiger-skin as a body covering elephant-skin and human skin cap and apron of carved human bones; vahana– lotus throne, shakti; two hands, in Yab-Yum position. Cf. Bunce, Fredrick W., op. cit., p. 584.

7. Tsogdag: The Tibetan equivalent of the Sanskrit for Ganesa. A Hindu god who has been accepted into the Buddhist pantheon and sometimes referred to as a Bighna. Another name for the deity Ganapati. Cf. Bunce, fredric W., *op. cit.,* p. 166.

8. Jigjed: In Sanskrit equivalent Yamantaka. He is the conqueror of the god of death. In his terrifying aspect Yamantaka is also known as Bhairava or Vajrabhairava ('Jigs byed or dpal rdo rje jigs byed–Pron. Pel Dorje jigje) and thus also appears to be related to Siva one of whose name is Bhairava (terrible). In Tibet Yamantaka is considered a ferocious emanation of Manjusri and he is the special Yidam of the Geluk-pa order, Cf. Finegan Jack; *op. cit.,* pp. 133-34.

9. Dorje Chang; Tibetan transliteral equivalent of the Sanskrit for Vajradhara. The tantric manifestation of Sakyamuni Buddha and anthropomorphic representation of Adi Buddha. When in the Yab-Yum pose with shakti. They represent that the distinction between "Duality and Oneness absolute". Face: one clam; arms: two vajrahimkara mudra with thunderbolt and ball; mudra vajrahumkara, legs two, Asana dhyanasana colour dark-blue or god ornaments; five leafted crown with tight necklace armlet wristlet bracelet anklet a warp for the lower body and one for the upper a garland to the thigh and one to the naval, a girdle (wide belt) and a sash; Shakti Prajraparmita form include karmavajra Dharmavajra and Yogambara with Shakti. Cf. Bunce Fredrick W. *op. cit..* p. 577.

10

Frescos in Old Dukhang

On 8th April 2006, I alongwith Lama Nangyal[1] came to Chamra of the Matho monastery[2] at about 6.30 A.M. Climbing the monastery was a tiresome task for me. Therefore, I took little rest at the varanda of old Dukhang. This Dukhang is also named as:

1. Tung-pa Dukhang
2. Tung-pa Dorje Dukhang } ⇒ (Dukhang Nying pa)

Therefore, it is clearly evident that the Dukhang was constructed by Tunghpa Dorje Palsang.[3]

In the meanwhile Lama Nangyal brought key of the said Dukhang from the comer. He opened the door, we entered into the Dukhang. It was a dark prayer hall in which two rows were assigned for Lamas, so that they could sit together and read religious texts during prayer. Here I saw many old and new wall paintings. Later with the help of Lama Nangyal I started my research work (Fig. 10.1).

Frescos

The Dkuhang has eight seats in each row and one throne for religious high rank Lama. Here follows the details of mural paintings.

1. Jamyang Mar-ser (Tib. 'again abyang dmar gser)

In Sanskrit language pronounced Manjusri.[4] It is red and yellow mixed colour fresco, located on the wall behind Rigsum Gonpo in peaceful form.

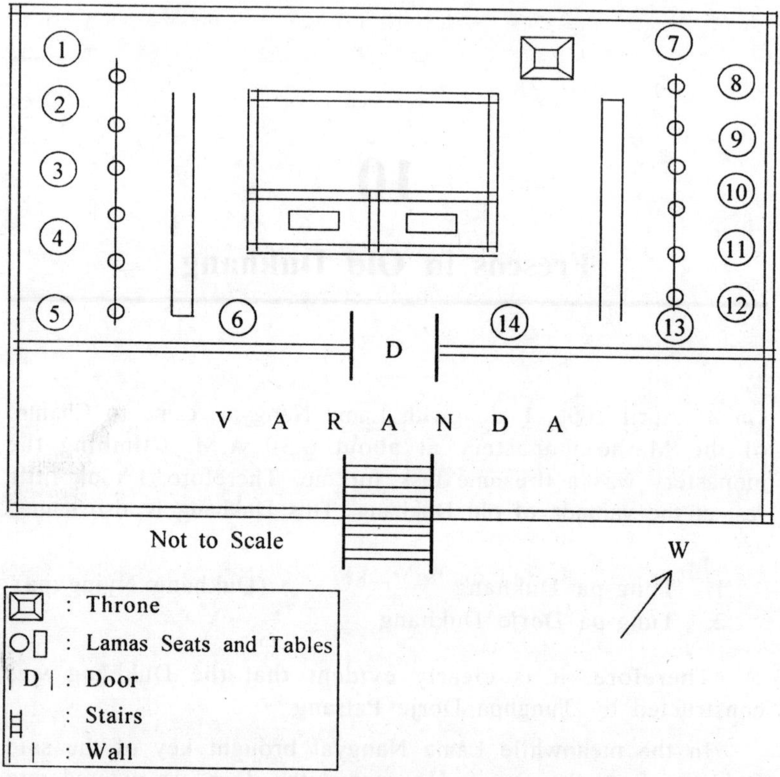

Fig. 10.1: Painting in Old Dukhang

Posture: Seated

Colour: Mar-Ser (Red & Yellow mixed)

Hand: Two : Sword & lotus flower

2. Lama Zusdak Rinchen:

Posture: Seated on throne

Dress: Lama dress i.e. Red Zang-gos (zang-dgos) for upper body and Chamse red.

Hand: Two

Left hand holds pen

Right hand carries Paper

Mandala: He is surrounded by Buddhist saints who are depicted in setting Posture. The details is listed below:

1. Virupa[5]:

Hat: Red

Cloths: Upper-Red

Lower-Yellow

Hands: Two; Right hand carries *Pothi*

2. Mela[6]:

Cloths: White

Asana: Seated on tiger skin

3. Not identified Fresco: It is surrounded by four Chosrgyal Phagspa

4. Not identified Fresco:

Posture: Seated on tiger skin

Cloths: Outer white.

Inner red.

Hair style: Like Yogi

5. *Paldan Choskyong:* (Tib. dpal ldan chos skyong)

Hat : Red

Dress: Outer red

Inner red

Holds: (i) Sword on lotus flower

(ii) Pothi

(iii) Vase

6. Rinchen Migyur Gyaltsen (Tib. rin chen mi agyur rgyal tsen)

Hat: Red

Dress: Upper-red

Inner- Yellow

Mudra: Dharmcakra

Holds: Pothi

7. Rinchen Choszot (Tib. rin chen chos mdzod)

Hat: Red

Dress: Red Lama cloths

Posture: Right hand holds pot

Left hand rest near heart

Mandala: Started from Left

(i) Paldan Choskyong

Dress: Up-Red

Down- Yellow

Mudra: Left hand in Abhaya; touches thumb by first finger

Right hand carries jewel

(ii) Unidentified Lama (Sakya Lama):

Dress: Outer-Red

Inner-Red

Mudra: Dhyan mudra carries (*Kalash or Pungpa* with plant.

(iii) Panchen Nagvang Kang-ga Ishes wangchuk (Tib. Pan chen ngag dang kung dga' a yi shes dbang-phyug)

Mudra: Left hand carries jewel

Right hand in Abhaya mudra

Dress: Outer- Red } ⇒ Lama dress
Inner- Red

Hat: Red

Second Row From up to Down:

(i) Jamyang Khencse (Tib. jam dbyangs mkhyen)

Mudra: Right arm holds Vajra, rests near heart

Left arm carries Pot

Dress: Upper- slight Yellow mixed red

(Tib. 'a zam-tse) chamse- red (to cover upper part of the body).

(ii) Kunga lotos (Tib. Kung dg'a blo gros)

Dress: Upper- slight Yellow mixed red
Chamse – Yellow

Hat: Red

Mudra: Dharmacakra

3. Norchen Kung-ga zang-po (Tib. ngor chen kun dg'a bzang po)

Centre fresco is the founder of Ngorpa, a sub sect of Sakya tradition

Posture: Seated
Right hand holds Vajra in flower.
Left hand holds bell with flower.

Hat: Red

Dress: Upper- Red
Lower- Slight yellowish

Mudra: Dharmacakra

Left side at the bottom

A standing Lama offering jewel and plant with white scarf

Right side at the bottom

A standing Lama offering jewel and plant with blue scarf

Offering Table (Left right):

(i) Pot of *nas*
(ii) White *damru*
(iii) Mirror
(iv) Skull
(v) Pungpa

Mandala: In the mandala of Norchen kung-ga zangpo the following frescos are depicted from right side

(i) kung-ga
Posture: Seated

Mudra: Right hand holds vajra
Left hand holds bell, rests near heart

Dress: Upper: Red

Inner: Red

(ii) Kung-ga gyaltsan:

Right side of kung-ga

Mudra: Dharmacakra; both hands carry flowers

Hat: Red

Dress: Upper- red

Lower – Yellow

Posture: Seated

Below the Kung-ga gyaltsan: Dadul Wangcuk (Tib. dgra' adul dbang phyng)

Holds: Arrow in his right arm.

Pungpa in his left arm.

Mudra: Right hand rests near heart

Dress: Upper – Red

Lower – Yellow

Hat: Red

Whole body is covered by Lama dress.

Below Dudul Wangcuk: Kung-ga Rinchen left hand is covered by white cloth; carries *pothi* in varada mudra

Dress: Upper- Red

Lower- Red

4. Verocana (Vairocana): Centre fresco

Colour of body- White

Height – 18"

Posture- Seated in Dhyan mudra; legs folded in meditation form.

Faces/ Heads – Four

Mandala: The following frescos are depicted in mandala of Verocana (or vairocana)

(i) Sakya Rigvang Serpo (Tib. Sa-skya-sigs- dbang bserpo)

Asana: Dhyanasana

Mudra: Preaching

Body Colour: Golden

Hair style: Similar to Yogi

Left to Centre Fresco in the Mandala:

(ii) Dorje Lchakdog

Ornaments: Both hands rest near heart

Body colour: Yellow mixed with red.

Posture: Seated

Dress: Upper- thin green shawl

Lower – upper blue with red robe

(iii) Below lchakdog: Dorje Chogkar Rung Zamar (Tib. Chogdkar la cung zet dmarba)

Asana: Dhyana

Mudra: Right hand near heart

Left hand holds flower plant

Body colour: White

Cloths: Upper part of body covered by a golden robe

Lower part red with upper blue cloth.

(iv) Dorje Snonpo Sngonpo (Tib. rdor rje snon po snon po)

Body colour: Blue

Mudra: Right hand holds sword

Left hand holds *pothi*, rest near heart

Dress: Thin red shawl for upper part

Lower –Red robe

Asana: Dhyana

(v) Dorje Gya Serpo (Tib. rdo-rje rgya gser po)

Body colour: Golden

Mudra: Right hand holds Cakra
Left hand rests near heart

Asana: Dhyana

Dress: Upper- Green robe
Lower-Red with upper blue robe

(vi) Dorje Mava Marser (Tib. rdo-rje smra ba dmar ser)

Mudra: Right hand holds blue dorje
Left hand rests near heart

Asana: Dhyana

Dress: Upper- Blue with red robe

(vii) Goskarmo

Body Clour: Golden

Mudra: Right hand holds plant
Left hand lies on Asana

Cloth: Upper- Blue with green
Lower –Red with Blue

Asana: Right leg folds
Left leg open outside

One head and two arms

(viii) Marme Ma:

Body colour: Slight pink

Mudra: Right hand holds chodme *(Prasad)*
Left hand rests left side near heart, holds last finger by thumb

Asana: Left leg folds
Right leg open

Dress: Upper- Red robe
Lower- Red upper blue robe

One head and two arms

(ix) Luma Karmar:

Body colour: White; holds *Sitar*

Hands: Two

Holds Sitar's lower portion by right hand, upper part by left hand;

Dress: Upper- Green robe

Lower – Red with Blue robe

Asana: Left leg open

Right leg closed

One head and two arms

(x) Mentok Chergi ljang Khu (Tib. Mentok cher gyas ljang khu)

Body Colour: Green

Mudra: Dhyana

Asana: Meditation

Hands: Left arm in Dhyana mudra

Posture Right arm in Abhaya

Dress: Upper-Red robe

Lower –Red with upper Blue

Head one and two arms

(xi) Dorje Las Snatesogs:

Body Colour: White

Dress: Upper- Green

Lower–Orange with blue robe

Hand Posture: Holds vajra gyatam in right hand, which rests near heart. Holds bell in left hand, has one head and two arms.

(xii) Ti Chamba Ljang Khu:

Body Colour: Green

Hand Posture: Dharmachakra holds *Sankha*

Dress: Upper blue

Lower red with blue.

Head one and arms two

(xiii) Dolma Zanku (Green Tara):[8]

Hands Posture: Right hand holds flower
Left hand lies on Asana

Asana: Left leg folds inside.
Right leg open free.

Dress: Upper- Orange shawl
Lower- Red with blue robe.

Head one and arms two.

(xiv) Srung Waserpo:

Body Colour: Yellow

Hands Posture: Holds robe by his hands near heart

Dress: Upper- Green robe
Lower- Red with blue.

Asana: Dhyana

Head one and arms two.

(xv) Dorje Tilbu Ma Ljang Khu:

Body Colour: Green

Hand Posture: Right hand holds bell, left hand holds vajra and rests on her left leg.

Asana: Seated; left leg open right leg closed.

Dress: Upper- Red robe.
Lower- Blue on red robe.

Head one and arms two

(xvi) Garma Ljang Khu:

Body Colour: Green

Hand Posture: Holds vajra in her right hand, left hand lies near left side of her heart, holds second finger showing with palm outside.

Asana: Right leg open
Left leg closed ⇒ (Dancing asana)

Dress: Upper- Red robe
Lower- Blue on red robe

Head one and arms two.

(xvii) Dorje Nod Jin Nakpo:

Body Colour: Blue black like Mahakala.

Hands Posture: Hold white scarf's both ends and lies near face.

Asana: Dhyana

Head one and arms two.

(xviii) Dorje Khu Tsur Serpo:

Body colour: Yellow

Hands Posture: Holds bell in right hand and vajra rte-lng pa in left; place both arms near her heart.

Asana: Dhyana

Head one and arms two.

(xix) Unidentified Just Below This Fresco Je Cum Idan Kharlo is Painted.

Body Colour: White

Posture: Holds flower in her left hand & right hand lies on her right thigh

Dress: Upper; Green robe
Lower: Blue on red robe

Asana: Dhyana

Head one and arms two.

From right side

(xx) Dorje Zyad pa Karpo (Tib. bzhad Pa Karpo)

Colour: White

Mudra: Right hand holds second finger, left hand holds second and third fingers (or Dharmacakra)

Asana: Dhyana

Garments: Green shawl for upper body and lower limbs are

covered by blue on red robe. Head one and arms two.

(xxi) Namkha Dog Chen:

Holds: *Chatari* in her right hands. Left hand in Dhyana mudra

Body Colour: Sky blue

Garments: Green shawl for upper body and covered lower limbs by blue on red robe.

(xxii) Dorje Rzizet Mar Ser:

Body Colour: Yellow & red mixed

Symbol & Mudra: Holds sun which is tied with thread in right hand; left hand lies on left thigh, palm turned upward

Asana: Dhyana

Garments: Upper body covered with red shawl and lower limbs are covered with blue on red.

Ornaments: Bodhisattva ornaments

Head: One

Hands: Two

(xxiii) Meok Ma Sermo:

Body Colour: Yellow

Symbol & Mudra: Hold flowers in her both hands

Asana: Right leg in usual position of like Buddha. Other leg pendant

Head: One

Hands: Two

Garments: Upper body is covered with green shawl and lower limbs by blue on red robe.

(xxiv) Dorje Rinchen Serpo:

Body colour: Yellow

Symbol & Mudra: Holds jewel in right hand, Ghanta (Tib. Til bu) in other hand left hand rests on left thigh

Garments: Covered upper body by blue shawl, lower limbs by blue on red robe.

Asana: Dhyanasana

(xxv) Mama Ki Snon Mo:

Body Colour: Blue

Symbol & Mudra: Holds vajra in right hands on right side of breast. The other hand rests on flower throne.

Garments: Green shawl for upper body, lower limbs are covered by blue on red robe.

Asana: Lalitasana- Left leg pendent. Other leg in usual position of a Buddha.

(xxvi) Dorje Threng Sermo:

Body Colour: Yellow

Symbol & Mudra: Holds *mala* in her both hands.

Garments: Green shawl for upper body, lower limbs is covered by blue on red robe.

Asana: Lalitasana – Left leg pendent, right in usual position of a Buddha.

(xxvii) Dorje Jags Pa Serpo:

Body colour: Yellow

Symbol & Mudra: Holds a chain in both hands.

Garments: Green shawl for upper body and lower part of her body is covered by blue on red robe

Asana: Lalitasana – Left leg pendent and right leg is usual position of a Buddha.

(xxviii) Dorje Lagpa Ljang Ku

Body Colour: Green

Symbol & Mudra: Bhutadamara holds third finger by both arms and placed in front of breast.

Asana: Dhyana

Garments: Wears blue scarf on upper body and covers lower limbs by blue on red robe.

(xxix) Gyal Chog Ring Chen Snon Po:

Body colour: Blue

Symbol & Mudra: Varada

Garments: Red shawl for upper body and lower limbs are covered with pink on red robe .

Asana: Dhyana

(xxx) Dhug Sposma:

Body colour: White

Symbol & Mudra: Holds incense (Tib. spos) by her both her arms.

Garments: Green shawl draped over one shoulder. Lower limbs are covered by blue on red.

Asana: Lalitasana – Left leg pendant and right left is usual position of a Buddha.

(xxxi) Dorje Chag Pa Marpo:

Body colour: Red

Symbol & Mudra: Left hand stretches Chapa & Sara (or bow and arrow) by right; symbol of Marici Kurukulla. Raktalokesvara and Mayajalakrama-ryavaloki-tesvara.

Garments: Wears blue scarf on upper body and lower limbs are covered by blue on red robe.

(xxxii) Chanma Karmo:

Body colour: White

Symbol & Mudra: Holds *Chakra* in her right hand on the right side of breast. The other rests on throne

Asana: Lalitasana- Left leg pendant and right in usual position of a Buddha.

Garments: Blue shawl draped over one shoulder. Lower limbs are covered by blue on red robe.

(xxxiii) Gegmo Karmo:

Body colour: White

Symbol & Mudra: Vajrahumkara, Buddha supreme and eternal, wrists crossed at breast, holding vajra and ghanta. Mudra of vajradhara, Samvara, Trailokyavijaya and Yidam forms of Dhyanibuddhas with Saktis.

Garments: Red shawl draped over one shoulder. Lower limbs are covered by blue on red robe.

Asana: Lalitasana – Left leg pendent and right in usual position of a Buddha.

(xxxiv) Dorje Gyalpo Serpo:

Body colour: Golden

Symbol & Mudra: Holds parasu (Tib lchak kyu) in his right hand and left Karana mudra; in right hand little finger and index finger are stretched against the palm or second and third fingers are crossed by thumb and rest near chest.

Garments: Green shawl draped over one shoulder, lower limbs are covered by blue and red robe.

Asana: Dhyana

(xxxv) Dorsen Karpo (White Vajrasattva):

Body colour: White

Symbol & Mudra: Vajrahumkara, Buddha supreme and eternal; wrists crossed at breast, vajra in his right hand and bell or ghanta in left.

Asana: Dhyana

Garments: Red shawl draped over one shoulder, lower limbs are covered by blue on red robe.

(xxxvi) Dorje Lchal Kyu Karpo:

Body colour: White

Symbol & Mudra: Right hand holds long chak-yu and left holds inner cloth.

Garments: Green shawl draped over one shoulder, lower limbs are covered by blue on red robe.

Asana: Lalitasana- Left leg pendent and right in usual position of a Buddha

(xxxvii) Jung-gyal Po (Tib. sbyong b'ai rgyal Po):

This fresco lies just below the centre fresco.

Symbol & Mudra: Dhyana

Garments: Green robe draped over one shoulder and lower limbs are covered by blue on red robe.

Asana: Dhyana

Body colour: White

Head: One

Hands: Two

Beside the above mandala, there are some more frescos near the door on right side. The details are listed below:

(i) Jung Po dul jet:

Body colour: Black & blue mixed similar to Gonpo (or Gompo) surrounded with flames.

Mudra: Wrathful form

(ii) Hey griva (Tib. rtandin)

Head –One

Arms- Four

Body colour: Orange mixed red

Symbol: Holds *gada* and flower; cakra and pasa. He steps to right

Mudra: Wrathful form

All the above frescos are being circled by painting of boundary wall alongwith gate.

Upper Side of the Centre Fresco

(i) Mithuk Pa (or Mi-hkhrugs- pa skt. Aksobhya):[9]

Body colour: Blue

Mudra & Symbol: Right hand bhumisparsha left hand in dhyana mudra holding vajra.

Asana: Dhayana

Face: One

Hands: Two

(ii) Sakyamuni Buddha[10]

Body colour: Golden

Mudra & Symbol: Right hand in bhumisparsha; left hand holds patra in Dhyana mudra

Asana: Dhyana

5. Chepakmet:[11]

Measurement: Hight- 3'

Main fresco

Body Colour: Red

Symbol & Mudra: Holds (Tib. Bumpa) or Pungpa with Dhyana mudra

Garments: Upper: Green shawl.

Lower: Blue on red robe.

Mandala: The following deities are depicted in the mandala

(i) Sakya Lama:

Mudra: Dharmacakra

Hands: Two

Garments: Red Lama dress

Head: One

Asana: Dhyana

(ii) Heygriva:[12]

Face: One, red colour with wrathful form.

Hands: Two

Symbol & Mudra: Holds Chakra in right hand, Left hand-ring finger touches thumb facing palm outside.

Posture: Standing

Garments: Lower limbs covered by tiger skin and upper by elephant skin.

Ornamanrs: Snake

(iii) Chagdor (Skt. Vajrapani)[13]*:*

Wrathful form

Body colour: Blue

(iv) Khyung:[14]

Body colour: Dark blue

Symbol & Mudra: Holds snake's head in his right hand tail in left, wrathful form with flames, head buffalo and face like parrot.

Body: Human

Legs: Eagel Tampted snake by his both legs. Snake head by right leg and tail by left.

Posture: Standing with streaches his wings, human body, head buffalo and bird legs all together is called Dagpo sum sdup.

(v) Rje tsun mi yo wa:

Body colour: Blue black

Symbol & Mudra: Wrathful form with flame like hairs holds sword in his left hand.

Garments: Wears tiger skin in lower limbs and upper by green shawl.

Ornaments: Bones garland

Posture: Standing

Right Side

(vi) Namgyal ma:[15]

Body Colour: White

Hands: Eight

Face: Three; including Centre white face, left blue-black and right golden.

Asana: Dhyana

Garments: Upper: Green shawl

Lower: Blue on red robe.

(vii) Jamyang:[16]

Hands: Four

Right hand- (i) Holds sword

(ii) Holds arrow

Left hands: (i) Pothi with flower

(ii) Bow

Asana: Dhyana

(viii) Kurukulla (Red Tara)[17]

Body colour: Red

Hands: Four; holds (i) Ankusa

(ii) Demon nus

(iii) Bow & arrow (Chapa & Sara)

Head: One

Posture: Standing

Eyes: Three

Mudra: Wrathful

Ornaments: Human skulls

Garments: Wears shawl on upper part of the body.

Lower – Tiger skin

Posture: Standing, left leg on human body; right leg up called Ardhaparyanka asana.

(ix) Tsog sdhak lang na

Hands: 12 which holds the following symbols.

Right hands: (i) Peacock feather

(ii) Sword with vajra

(iii) Parasu

(iv) Arrow

(v) Pharsa with vajra

(vi) Katika rests near chest

Left hands:

(i) Trishul

(ii) Skull

(iii) Three skulled Trisul

(iv) Bow

(v) Thread

(vi) Skull cup rests near chest

Posture: Standing strup below moose, right leg up folds parallel earth; Ardhaparyanka asana.

(x) Yum Chenmo (Skt. Mahamaya)

This fresco is on the wall of the Dukhang at the east along the door.

Hands: Four

Body colour: Golden

Symbol & Mudra:

Right hands hold:

(i) Mala

(ii) Vajra

Left hands hold:

(i) *Pothi*

(ii) Pot *(Patra)*

Garments: Upper body is covered by green shawl lower limbs by blue on red robe.

Asana: Dhyana

Kurukulla, Tsogdak and Yum chenmo all together is called Marpo skar sum.

(6) Gonpo (Mahakala)

Name: Dandi Mahakala

Posture: Seated

Hands: Two

Body colour: Blue-Black

Mandala: The following deities are depicted in his mandala.

Left from Upper Side Towards Down: On Ist Row

(1) Bata Nagpo:

Colour: Blue-Black

Garments: Whole body is covered with tiger skin, Belt-blue scarf.

Ornaments: Human hands garlands; bones bangles

Posture: Standing, wrathful

Hands: Two; right hand holds vajrakila and left skull cup.

(2) Dhod Kham Wangchukma

Colour: Blue-Black

Vahana: Mala (Tib. Tiu); colour white mixed brown

Hands: Four; Right hands hold

(i) sword

(ii) skull cup lies near hear;

Left hands hold

(i) Trishul

(ii) 2nd finger hold upwards

Ornaments: Human heads and bones garlands human skin, snake and white dog skin

Hair Style: Hair in flame

Mudra: Wrathful with flame

(3) Nagmo nodjin yum:

Mudra: Wrathful with flame

Garments: Brown

Garland: Human heads and bones

Posture: Standing

Symbol: Right hand holds karttrika, left holds skull cup filled with blood and orange colour flames

Eyes: There to see human body by his eyes with left step up

(4) Pata (or Bata)

Mudra: Wrathful, standing with greenish flames.

Colour: Blue- Black

Hands: Holds sword in his right hand, left hand holds skull cup filled with blood.

Ornaments: Human bones garment.

Eyes: Three

Garments: Blue scarf for upper body.

IInd Row from Upper Towards Down

(v)'akajati (Ekajata)[18]

Mudra & Symbol: Wrathful; Karttrka and Kapala.

Colour: Blue – Black

Hands: Two; holds parasu (Khadga) in his right hand and other hand rests near breast.

Garments: White shawl for upper body and tiger skin for lower limbs.

Posture: Seated rajalila asana.

(vi) Mag zor ma

Vahana: Mule, white and brown colour

Mudra: Wrathful

Symbol: Right hand holds sword which both heads like dorje, left hand holds skull cup filled with blood.

Ornaments: Bones garland, and snake necklece which is a symbol of Buddha. The fresco is in a ring of brown, white and red flames.

(vii) Nag Po nodjin yap:

Mudra: Wrathful

Vahan: Tibetan white lion

Ornaments: Snake and bone garland

Eye: Three

Hands: Holds skull cup filled with blood by his left and right hand sword

Colour: Yellow

The fresco is in a sign of yellow flames.

(viii) Sring mo ral chig ma:

Mudra: Wrathful

Garments: Brown robe

Colour: Blue–Black

Hands: Two holds *cakyu* in his right hand and chain in left.

Eyes: Three

Leg: Two; trampling a human by his left leg, right step up.

In the middle of Puta and Sring mo ral chig ma

Black Women:

Colour: Black

Hands: Two; holds dorje in her right hand and skull cup in left.

Below the Gonpo Dandi from Left to right

(i) Geylong

Hands: Two; holds *kharsil* in his right hand and *lunze* in left

Posture: Standing

Garments: Red cap, Orange colour *chosgos* for upper body and red *shantap*

(ii) *Offerings:* Blood, nose, eye, ear human heads etc.

(iii) *Pudmed (girl)*: White cloth for her lower limbs

(iv) *Skyes Pa:* He is a symbol of soldier; holds sword and *dhal*; weared chain garments.

(v) *Janak:* Weared black cap, holds Vajrakila in his right hand, skull, cup in left; blue garments, Dor-gang-green pangkhep- green in the middle red colour

Right side of the Gonpo dandi (the Centre fresco) Ist Row From upper side towards down.

(i) Lasgon:

Colour: Blue-Black

Hands: Two; holds karttrka in his right hand and skull cup filled with blood in his left.

Eyes: Three

Crown: Five skull

Ornaments: Human heads and bones

Garments: Tiger skin

Leg: Two; trampling a human.

Mudra: Wrathful with yellow flames

(ii) Dram Zuk

Colour: Light blue

Hands: Two; holds skull cup in right hand, lies in the middle and sword at the arm- pit; left hand holds *kangling* (it is made of human thigh bone)

Ornaments: All are made of human bones

Eyes: Three

Legs: Two trampling human body left

Offerings: Left thigh, vajra, karttrka, skull cup & patra (pot).

Garments: Green shawl for upper body; white, red and orange Pangkhep for lower part of the body. Below to the above frescos four naked dancing girls hold skull cup and karttrka.

(iii) Zal zi pa dram zei zug tsan

Mudra: Wrathful with flames

Hands: Two; right hand holds Vajra; left hand rests near his chest, holds skull cup filled with blood.

Posture: Standing

Eyes: Three

Crown: Cotpan

IInd row from upper side towards down.

(iv) Jigjet (Yamantaka): ? (or may chosgyal)

Colour: Blue - black

(v) Turdak (Chitipiti or Citipati):

Mudra: Two citipati or skeletons with arms interlaced, dancing the Tsam dance on corpse.

Hands: Each has two hands; both carry wands with skull tops, one holds a kapala and the other a kalasa.

Garments: Green & Blue scarfs for upper body, lower limbs also have same colour.

Posture: Both standing on one leg, right turdak folds up right leg and left turdak folds up left leg.

(vi) Chagdor (Vajrapani):

Colours: Dark blue

Hands: Two holds vajra in right hand.

Posture: Standing

Wall on the Door: Left & Right Side

(i) Vajrapani:

Colour: Dark blue

Posture: Standing

Hands: Two; holds vajra in right hand

(ii) Avalokitesvara:

Colour: White

Asana: Standing

Mudra & Symbol: Namaskara mudra; made symbols and padma.

(iii) Manjusri:

Asana: Standing

Colour: Yellow

Mudra: Dharmacakra; holds stems of Padma, with flowers at shoulders level supporting khadga and *pustaka.*

Frescos Behind Bum Pothi

Vajra Guru (Padmasambhav):[19]

Cap: Red

Symbol & Mudra: Trishul in arm-pit at his left hand holds skull cup with jewel and plant. Dhyana mudra right hand holds vajra, rests near his heart.

Garments: Red camse (Tsen-tṣe), orange Chos-gos, blue robe, green belt or scarf

Asana: Standing.

Offering ladies: Two ladies standing right and left side of Padmasambava offering prayer. They are his consorts called mandarva and Eshy Tsogyal.

Frescos on Left Wall of the Dukhang

(8) Sachan Kunga Nying po

Asana: Dhyana

Symbol & Mudra: Right hand holds flower left hand in varada mudra

Garments: Without cap, yellow with red robe for upper body and brown chosgos tied with blue scarf.

Position: This is the main or centre fresco and has the following deities in his mandala.

(i) Lopon sodnam rtse mo:

Location: Right side of the Centre fresco

Mudra: Dharmacara

Asana: Seated

Garments: Blue robe for upper part of the body and brown chosgos tied with yellow scarf.

Below the Lopon Sodnam rtse mo

(ii) Rtseun rinpoche dag Pa gyaltsen

Hands: Holds vajra in right hand rests near chest. Tilbu in his left hand rests on his thigh at the centre.

Garments: Blue robe for upper part of the body and red chosgos with yellow scarf.

Below the (ii)

(iii) Pal namo

Mudra: Dharmacakra

Garments: Cap red Chosgos- Red

(iv) Sakya Pandita

One saint stretches up his left hand, standing near his head in the fresco.

Left side up to down

(v) Sakya Lama:

Garments: Cap- Red

Chosgos- Red

Symbol & Mudra: Right hand holds sword with flowers, left hand holds flower

Asana: Dhyana

Mudra: Dharmacakra

Below Sakya Lama:

(vi) Chosgyal Phagspa:

Mudra: Dharmacakra

Hands: Two; holds jewel in left hand

Asana: Latitvasana.

Garments: Cap-Red

Chosgos-Red

(vii) Sa-kya Pandita:

Garments: Cap-Red

Chosgos-Red

Mudra: Dharmacakra

Symbol: Sword with flower in his right hand and flower with pothi in left hand.

9. Gyalva Lobzang Dragpa:

Mudra: Dharmachakra; holds sword with flower in right hand; left hand holds pothi with flowers, wear yellow cap.

Asana: Dhyana

Mandala: The following deities are depicted in the Gyalva lozang Drag pa (Tsongkhapa) mandala.

Right Side

(i) Gyal sabje:

Mudra: Dharmacakra

Symbol and posture of hand: He is standing at the left of centre Tsongkhapa, holds lunze in his right hand and *pothi* in left hand.

Garments: Red robe for upper part of the body and lower limbs covered by yellow robe.

(ii) Khadubje:

He is standing at the right of Tsongkhapa.

Symbol & Mudra: Dhamacakra mudra, holds lungze in his right hand and *pothi* in left hand.

Garments: Red robe for upper part of the body, lower limbs covered by yellow robe.

Right Side above tsong-khapa

(iii) Geluk-Pa Lama:

Garments: Cap –Yellow

Chosgos- Red

Camse (Tib. Tsanse) – Red

Mudra: Dharmcakra; with pothi in his left hand

Below Geluk-Pa Lama

(iv) Atisa:[20]

Mudra: Dharmacakra

Garments: Cap-Red [Monsatic robes]

Chosgos-Red

Santap-Red

Left upper side Tsong-Khapa

(v) Gelukpa Lama Gye dhun dup

Garments: Cap- Yellow

Chosgos-Red

Santap-Red

Mudra: Left hand in Dhyana mudra and right in Bhumisparsha

Below Gye dhun dup

(vi) Khaduje, a Gelukpa Lama

Garments: Cap- Yellow

Chosgos-Red

Camse- Yellow

Hands: Two; holds *pothi* in left hand which rests on his lap.

Upper side adjacent to Gye dhun dup

(viii) Jam gon tashis

Mudra: Bhumisparsha

Hands: Two; left hand holds pothi

Garments: Chosgos-Red

Camse- Red

10. Sakya Pandita

Position: Central fresco

Mudra: Dharmacakra

Symbol: Asoka (flower) with lunze and Dharmachakra

Garments: Cap-Red

Chosgos-Red

Mandala: The following frescos are depicted in his mandala.

Right side up

(i) Sangyas Phunchog

Mudra: Dramcakra holds vajra in his right hand and left hand in Dhyana mudra.

Garments: Red shawl for upper and red robe for lower limbs.

Asana: Dhyana; seated on flower plant.

Next to Sangyas Phunchog (From left onwards)

(ii) Jamyang Sangyas

Mudra: Dharmacakra; holds lungze in his left hand; right hand in Dharmacakra.

Garments: Cap-head

Chosgos- Red

Camse- Red

Below Jamyang Sangyal

(iii) Chamba Sodnam Zangpo

Mudra: Dhyana

Garments: Cap-red

Chosgos- red

Camse- Yellow

Below Chamba Sodnam Zangpo

(iv) Namkha sandup

Mudra: Right hand in Dharmacakra mudra

Left hand holds jewel with Dhyana mudra.

Garments: Cap-red

Chosges- red

Camse- Yellow

11. Medicine Buddha (Tib. sangs- rgyas-sman-gyi-bla-Byduriyai-hod-kyi-rgyal-po Skt. Bhaisa- jyaguau)

Position: Centre fresco

Colour: Blue

Garments: Red in colour

Hands: Two; left hand holds lunze with dhyana mudra; right hand in varada with plant.

Mandala: In the mandala the following frescos are depicted

Left side up

(i) Kun Khyen pat kar:

Mudra: Right hand in Varada left hand holds flower plant.

Garments: Cap-red

Chosgos- red

Cemse- red

Next to Kun Khyed Pat ker (in left side)

(ii) Ngaganwang namgyal (Nawang Namgyal)

Mudra: Right hand in Bhumisparsha mudra left hand in Dhyana with pot *(patra)*

Garments: Cap-red. He has long beard and seems to be like a Lama of Drigung pa order.

12. Arya Avalokitesvara:

Hands: Four

Colour: White

Symbol & Mudra: Right hand holds *Mala* and left hand holds padma; the rest two hands in namaskar mudra.

Mandala: In the mandala the following frescos are depicted right side of Avalokitesvara.

(i) White Tara

Colour: White

Symbol & Mudra: Right arm in Varadata mudra, other in Vitarka with padma at left shoulder.

Asana: Dhyana

Garments: Red on blue scarf for upper part of her body. The lower limbs are covered with blue on red robe.

Below white Tara

(ii) Singe da:

Symbol & Mudra: Holds trishul with snake in her right hand; left hand lies on asana with flower and sword.

Vahana: Lion (Tibetan White Lion)

Nagins: Two females Nag loka deities seemed me as they are offering prayer, in front of them one green snake is depicted.

Left side of Avalokitesvara (Upper side to down wards)

(i) Jigrten gonpo: a Lama of Drigung pa order

Symbol & Mudra: Right hand in Bhumisparsha, left in meditation with pot.

Garments: All upper and lower robes are red.

Asna: Seated on flower plant

Below Jigrten Gonpo

(ii) Dolzang (Green Tara):

Mudra: Vitarka and varada mudras; utpala at shoulder.

Colours: Green

Asana: Lalit asana; lotus asana supporting right foot.

Below Green Tara

(iv) Tsering ma:

Vahan: Tibetan White lion

Symbol & Mudra: Holds vajra in her right hand and pot in left hand. The left hand rests near her heart.

13. Namsras terdhak gyat

Position: Centre fresco

Vahan: White Tibetan lion

Colour: Golden

Symbol & Mudra: Holds *thuk* in right hand. It rests near heart. Other hand holds magoose, units jewels.

Posture: Seated

Mandala: There are Buddhisattvas riding on eight horses depicted as they are taking part in war. All carry magooses and jewel, sword, pot etc.

Above the Centre Fresco

(i) Vajrapani: Wrathful form

Head: One

Hands: Two

Colour: Blue- black

14. Tam Chan Chosgyal

Body: Blue-black

Eyes: Three eyes

Crown: Five skull

Garlands & Belt: Human heads or skull or freshly severed heads and bones.

Symbol & Mudra: Right hand holds Khatvanga, left holds diamond robe.

Face: One, fierce.

Legs: Two trampling a human and mahe.

Left side of Tam chan Chosgyal

A female deity, colour-light blue; carries skull cup in her left hand and trishul (trident) in right; brown hair with flames and five skull crowns.

Frescos in Namling of old Dukhang

There some Indian Acharyas and Lama alongwith Sakyamuni Buddha are depicted on walls. Here follows further details (Fig. 10.2).

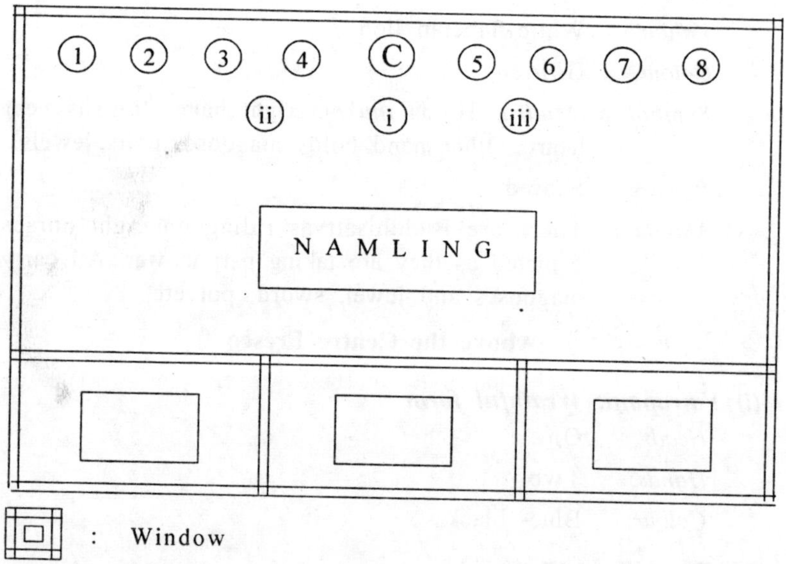

Fig. 10.2: Painting in Namling of Old Dukhang

Ist row against the window

(i) Sakyamuni Buddha: Centre fresco.

Asana: Meditation

Mudra: Right hand in Bhumishparsha; left hand with pot lunze in Dhyana mudra.

At the right and left sides Sariputra and Maudgalyayana are standing.

Left and right of Centre fresco

1. Klu sgrub

2. Thog med
3. 'aphags Pa lha
4. dbyig gnyen
5. phyegs glang
6. chos grags
7. yon tan' od
8. shakya'od (Indian Pandits) (Tib.ryyan phyogs gnyis)

IInd row against the window

(i) Gong ma nam nga: Centre fresco

Garments: Cho-gos- blue robe and inner white.

(ii) Unidentified Lama: It is at the right of centre fresco.

Cap: Brown

Mudra: Right hand in Dharmacakra and left in Dhyana with pothi.

Asana: Dhyana

(iii) Unidentified Lama:

Mudra: Both hands near his chest in Dharmacakra mudra.

Cap: Brown

To sum up, it is remarkable to note that the old Dukhang of Matho monastery has many old new frescos. They are the mixture of Bodhirattva and tantric Buddhist deities. The Boddhisattva frescos are in maximum number. Besides we may see some Lamas in wall paintings. They belong to Sakya tradition. Like all big monasteries this Dukhang has four lokpalas viz. Sbyan mig bzang and yul 'akhor srung are on the right side of door whereas 'aphags kyes Pa and rnam thos sras are depicted on the other side along the door of the Dukhang.

NOTES & REFERENCES

1. Lama Nangyal: He is a senior Lama student of Central Institute of Buddhist Studies, Choglamsar, Leh-Ladakh.
2. Matho monastery; Tib. Mangtro Monastery. According to the Tibetan tradition it is actually known as thubstan sheling chokhor.

3. Tungpa Palzang Dorje: He was a Saskya (Sakya) scholar Lama and the founder of the monastery.
4. Manjusri: Tib. Jam dbyangs Pron. Jamyang; and is shown in yellow, white, red black and blue forms; beautifully handsome young mahabodhisattva and bodhisattva and god of wisdom, science and agriculture. He is considered by the Northern Boddhisattva. With his sword he destroys ignorance and darkness, and frequently shown with Dhyani Bodhisattva, Avalokitesvara and Dhyani Budhisattva Vajrapani. These three together are known in Ladakh as 'Rig sum Gonpo;. They are mostly symbolized by red, white, and blue chortens. In Ladakh 'Rig Sum Ganpo' are carried in the form of Stupas, placed then on the gate of the Buddhist house. Cf. Bruce, Fredrick W: *An Encyclopaedia of Buddhist Deities, Demigods, Godlings, Saints and Demons,* Vol. I, D.K. Printworld Ltd. New Delhi; 1994; 331.
5. Virupa: In Sanskrit equivalent virupa, a Mahsidha.
6. Mela: (or Je Mila Tib. rje mi la): One of eighty Mahasiddhas saints and miracle wcrkers. They are the great tantric o: Mahayanism, the Mahagurus and "Root Lama".
7. Varocana (or Vairocana): Tib. rnam-par-snag-mdaz, rnam -par-snam- mded; Phon. Eng. Nampar Nangdze; shortened form; Nam-snan, Pron, Eng, Namnang meaning "Sun scion". A Dhyani Buddha whose dominion is the centre of the world. His recognition symbol is the wheel. Winter is his season. He is generally depicted with one calm face; two arms, holds wheel by his hands in Dharmachakra mudra; two legs; Asana in Dhrmacakra; White colour; vahana–pair of dragons; shakti- Locana or Tara; other forms are: Asokakanta, Arya Marici, Arya vajravarahi, Chunda, Dasabhujasita Marici, Grahamatrika, Mahasahasrapramardani, Maricipicuva Namasangiti, Sanksipta-Marici, Sitatapatra-Aparajita, ubhayavarahanana, Ubhayavarahanana-Marici, Usnisavijay, Vairocanabhisambodhi. Cf. Bruce, Frederic W.; *op cit.,* 11-12 & Batchelor, Stephen, *The Tibet Guide,* Wisdom Pub,. London, 1987; pp. 323-24.
8. Dolma Zanku (Green Tara): Tib. sgrol ma ljang gu, Pron. Drolma, Jang gu or green saviorese is probably the form of Tara incarnate in wencheng, the Chinese wife of king Songtsen Gonpo. She is green sits in the royal posture on the moon disc and lotus flower, her right leg extended, with its foot resting on a small lotus blossom. Cf.. Finegan, Jack, Tibet: A Dreamt of Image, Tibet House, New Dehi, 1986, 136.

9. Mithukpa (Skt. Aksobhya); The other forms Vajrasana, right hand is in bhumisparsa mudra; left hand is in dhyana mudra with vajra in plam or lying on throne before him. In Yi-dan form- Sakti Locana, Buddha. Symbol- Ghanta and vajra; Sakti symbol-Kapala and vajra; colour- Blue; Asana-Yab-yum dhyana. Cf. Gordon, Antoinette, K: *The Iconography of Tibetan Lamaism;* Munshiram Manoharlal Pub., 1998: 52&86.
10. Sakyamuni Buddha: The Buddha of the present age. He practised all kind of Buddhirattva's activities for countless asana to attain perfect enlightenment.
11. Chepakmet: Skt . Amitabha: The other forms are Both hands in dhyana mudra holding a patra, red colour, Dhyana Asana, Peacock Vahana, Sakti- Pandara; Yidam form – Budhha symbols- Ghanta and patra; Sakti symbols; kapala and karttika or ratna; Colour; yellow; Asana–Yab-yum dhyana. In heruka; Padmaheruka. Cf. Gordon, Antoinette K; *op. cit.,* 52, 86 & 87.
12. Heygriva: (or Hayagriva); The other forms are: One head, four arms. Holds gada and flowers; Cakra and paisa. He steps to right. Three hands four arms, two or four legs. Steps to right on demons. Holds vajra and flower; Capa and sara. He has a horse's head in his hair. Three heads, six arms, eight legs. Steps to right on nagas. Holds vajra, pasa, trishula; khadga, flag, and flames. He has three horse heads in hair. Three heads eight arms. Central head red and smiling; second head blue, with protruding tongue; third head, white biting lips. Hands hold vajra, padmam capa sara, gada, flower. There heads eight arms four legs; steps to eight on persons. Holds Cakra, Parasu and flower; Khadga, pasa and Kapala. He has horse heads in hair. He is in yab-yam with sakti who has one head and two arms. Cf. Gordon, Antoinette K. op. cit. p. 90.
13. Chagdor (Skt, Vajrapani): Acharayavajrapani. Blue; has the third eye sets to right; Dharmapala ornaments; fierce expression; serpent necklace; fierce expression; serpent necklace belt of heads; aureole of blames; in which there are sometimes garudas; uplifted eight hand holds vajra, left hand generally holds the pasa. Cf. Gardon, Antoinette K; *op cit.* 62.
14. Khyung: Vajrapani form of Garuda. He is standing dark blue has wings and claws of a garuda sometimes the beak. He stands on a dying naga. He holds a karttrka and a kalasa or has his two hands in namadkar mudra Cf. Gordon . Antoinettew. K., op cit. 95

15. Namgyal ma: Skt. Vajaya. The deity of longevity. She has got three faces each face shown mild anger; carries a vase filled with pills of longevity. Among the right hands the first hand holds a cross vajra near her heart the second holds a state of Amitabha on a white lotus. The third holds an arrow and the fourth is in boon-bestowing (varada) posture. The first left hand in meditation with an arm. The second is in compassionate with a rosary of vahra near the heart the third holds a bow and fourth is in fearless posture. There is a radiate disco of light around her heads. She is in Dhyana mudra seated on lotus flower.
16. Jamyang Skt. Manjusri: He is the embodiment of the wisdom of all the Buddhas and a Boddhisattva for the welfare of all sentient being. He was one of the main disciples of Sakyamuni who used to raise questions concerning the emptiness for the benefit of all listeness. He is the sole deity of wisdom.
17. Karukulla (Red Tara): The other form has one head, six or eight arms. Dances on corpses. Has the third eye and fierce expression, tantric symbols were Dharmapala ornaments and garments. Cf. Gardon, Antoinette K. *op cit.*, p. 76.
18. 'akajati (Ekajata): One hand, two arms. Seated in royal way, holds a karttrka and kapala. Wears Bodhisattva ornaments and garments. Caturbhuja- One hand four arms. Pratyalidhasana. She has the third eye. Right hands hold khadga and kapala, upper left hand holds disc and lower left is in vitarka mudra. Wears Budhisattva ornaments and garment. Angry forms-
    (i) One head, four arms. Angry. Pratyali- dhasana. Right hands holds kapala and churiwhite left hands holds kapala and utpala or chapa and sara and khadga and severed heads. She wears Dharmapala ornaments and garments;
    (ii) One head eight arms Angry. Right hands hold khadga, Sara vajra, churi; left hands hold capa, utpala parasu, kapala. Wears dharmapala ornaments and garments;
    (iii) Twelve heads, twenty-four arms. Tramples on gods, pratylidhasana. Has tantric and non-Tantric symbols. Has ferocious appearance is blue with red chignon. Wears Dharmapala ornaments and garments. Cf. Gardon, Antoinotte K,. *op. cit.* p. 76.
19. Vajra Guru Padmasambhava: Tib. Lopon Rinpoche. "Lotus Born One." an Indian Tantric invited by king Trisong Deten in the eighth Century A.D. He brought Buddhist Tantra in Tibet, subdued the local deities and demons while constructing the first Samyas

monastery in Tibet. He helped Santaraksita in his works on Buddhism in Tibet. During his reign Buddhism was amazingly spread throughout in Tibet. Hence he was recognised by Tibetan as the second Buddha.

20. Atisa: He helped to revive Buddhism in Tibet during 11th Century; and is one of the 84 Mahasiddhas.

11

Statues in Old Dukhang (Tib. Dukhang Nying)

It is remarkable to note that there are only a few Buddhist statues in this hall. An elaborate description is presented below. (Fig. 11.1)

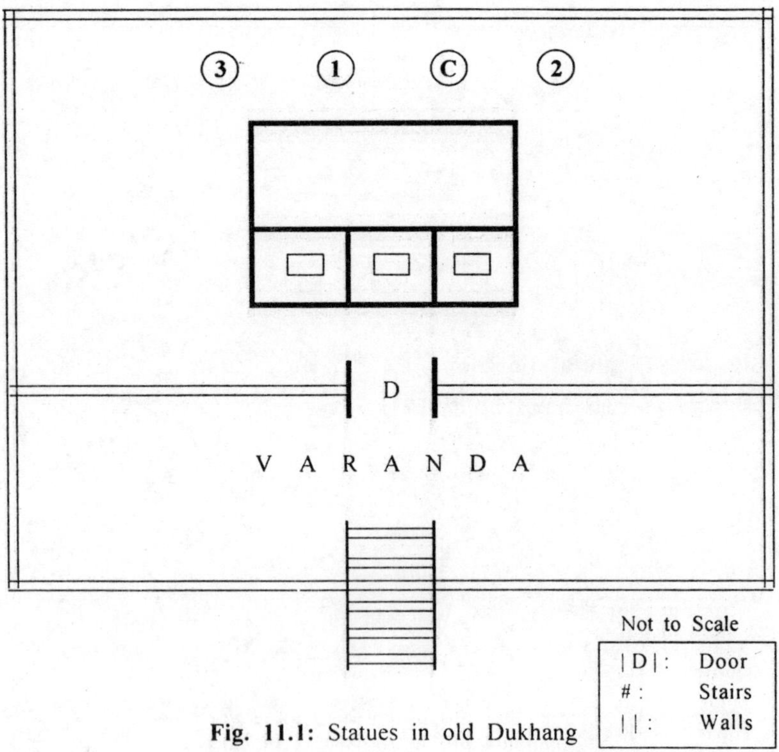

Fig. 11.1: Statues in old Dukhang

C. **Avalokitesvar:**[1]

Eyes: One thousand

The eight main arms hold the following symbols

Ist left and right hands in namaskar mudra.

Right hands hold:

IInd- Rosary

IIIrd- Cakra

VIth- Varada mudra

Left Hands hold:

IInd- Flower

IIInd- Bow & arrow

VIth- Patra (Pot)

Posture: Standing

Ornaments: Necklaces: (1) Gold kau, Ladakhi ornament

(2) Gold chain, a Ladakhi traditional ornament

Faces: Eleven faces, at the top Amitabha.

Height - 5'

Right side of Avalokitesvara

Sakyamuni Buddha [2]*:*

Mudra: Bhumisparsha

Symbols: Left hand holds lunze (Pot)

Height: 4½'

Posture: Seated

Body colour: Golden

Sariputra: Spiritual son standing on the right of Buddha

Maudgalyayana: Spiritual son standing on the left of Buddha

Both Sariputra and Maudgalayayan wear red garments.

Left Side of Avalokitesvara

Varocana (Vairocana)[3]

Height: 4'

Mudra: Dharmacakra

Colour: Golden (But in painting usually depicted in white)

Symbol: Cakra

Asana: Dhyana

Rigsum Gonpo Peaceful Form

They are at the right of Buddha statue

Avalokitesvara: Centre statue

Height: 5½'

Vajrapani:[4] Left to Avalokitesvara

Height: 3'

Jamyang:[5] Right to Avalokitesvara

Height: 3'

In this Dukhang there are seats in four rows for lamas, who on every especial occasions offer prayer.

Rogia and Pnkects (Tib. Ro brgya and Pang khyobs)

In this Dukhang I saw some ritual objects which are listed below:

(1) Nga[6]
(2) Tung[7]
(3) Sankha
(4) Rolmo[8]
(5) Five Dhvajas[9]
(6) Kapan[10] with eight pillars
(7) One Ludingkhan[11]

Room behind the Dukhang

There is a store room behind the Dukahng in which masks of different Buddhist god and goddesses are well preserved.

Throne

The two thrones of this Dukhang are:

1. Throne for Rinpoche.
2. Throne for a lama who direct or control the discipline during prayers.

Orders Chart

To maintain discipline in the gonpa, head lama issued orders, written in black ink on two cloth pieces, hanged through the pillars.

NOTES AND REFERENCES

1. *Avalokitesvara:* Tib. Changrezi (Chak-tong chen-tong). Bodhisattva who once took a vow to save all beings from suffering, when he realised the magnitude of his task his head exploded into countless pieces. His body was reassembled by Amitabha and the Bodhisattva Vajrapani into much more powerful form. The other story relates that once Avalokitesvara looked down upon the many beings in need of deliverance in the hell of Yama, the god of death, his head broke into ten pieces out of his great compassion these were later put together by his spiritual father Amitabha; thus in the figure there are nine gentle faces arranged in three tiers of three each, above that one wrathful face and at the top, the head of Amitabha. Cf. Bunce, Fredrick W.: *'An Encyclopaedia of Buddhist Deities, Demigods, Godlings, Saints and Demons,'* Vol. I, D.K. Printworld Ltd., New Delhi; 1994: 36.
2. *Sakyamuni Buddha:* He descended to the earth in 6th century and propogated Buddhism after attaining enlightenment. He delivered religious sermons for the benefit of all sentient beings travelling from one place to another till the end of his life. His central teaching is based on Prajnaparamita in which prajna (wisdom) and Upaya (method) are being explained. Cf. Sakyamuni: *An Exhibition of Rare Thankas;* CIBS, Leh; 2001: 20.
3. *Varocana (Verocana):* Yidam form-Sakti-Vajradhat-Visvari; Buddha symbols - Ghanta and Cakra; Sakti symbols-Kapala and churi; colour - White, Asana- yab-yum dhyana. Cf Gardon, Antoinette K.; *The Iconography of Tibetan Lamaism,* Mushiram. Manoharlal Pub., New Delhi, 1998:86.
4. *Vajrapani:* Mudra and symbol: Both hands in dhyana mudra;

vajra in palm. Dark blue in colour; Vitarka and varada mudras, surya and pustaka, Legs are loosely locked, flower is in right hand, left hand is in abhaya mudra; Right hand holds flowers in which is a sun-disk; left hand is in varada mudra; Left hand holds stem of padma, from which khadga rises; both hands are in vitarka mudra. In all the forms Vajrapani is in seated form. Cf. Gardon, Antoinette K., *op. cit.*: 60.

5. *Jamyang:* He is the embodiment of the wisdom of all the Buddhas, desended to the world as a Bodhisattva for the welfare of all sentient beings, and recognised as a sole deity of wisdom who blesses the devotees to sharpen their memory and intellect. As a result, a devotee can penetrate the vast and profound meanings of the Buddha's teachings. Buddhists believe that without the blessings of Manjusri, no body can develop the realization of the emptiness (shunyata) Cf. *Sakyamuni: An Exhibition of Rare Thankas; op. cit.*: 22.
6. Nga: It is a musical instrument used by lamas.
7. *Tung:* It is a musical instrument used by lamas in the monastery.
8. *Rolmo:* It is a musical instrument used by lamas during ritual prayers.
9. *Five Dhvajas:* Religious flags of Buddhist tradition.
10. *Kapan:* Different cloths used to cover the pillars of the monastery is called Kapan.
11. Ludingkan: He is 9 head lama of Sakya sect.

12

Mural Paintings in New Dukhang

On 9th April 2006 once again I along with Lama Namgyal entered in the chamra of Matho monastery. We arrived 8 O' clock in the morning. The Pujari (Priest) of the New Dukhang was in his room. Lama Namgyal went and brought key. After some time we climbed up through stairs and came in the Dukhang, and started the research work on frescos. An elaborate description is presented hereinafter (Fig. 12.1).

Left side of the Door

1. Tung pa dorje Palzang:[1] Cente Fresco

Height-3'

Width (from the centre of the chest): 2' 11"

Garments: Shawl for lower limbs is red and same colour scarf for upper body.

Mudra: Right hand in Bhumisparsha.

Left hand in Dhyana mudra.

Posture: Seated.

The following frescos are depicted in the mandala of Tungpa Dorje Palzang.

Right down to Centre fresco:

(1) Rong tsan kar po:[2]

Height: 1' 10"

Width: 1' 5"

Vahan: White horse

Mudra: Wrathful; holds small dhvaja of five colour cloth pieces with small mirror called Dadar in his left hand; right hand holds *sankha*.

Garments: Warlike golden cloths with white cloth.

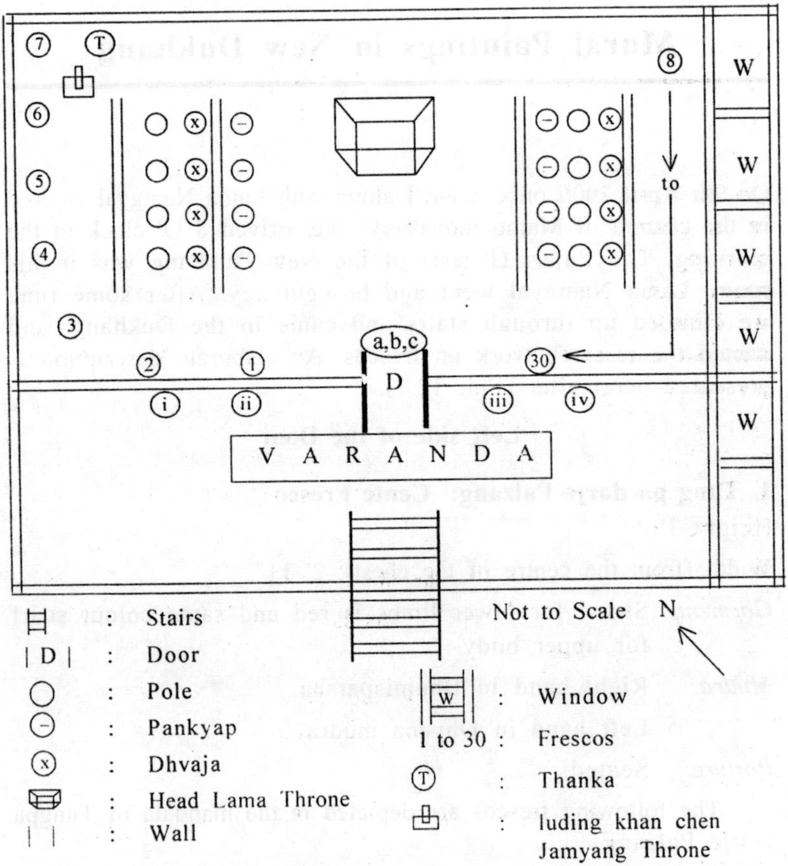

Fig. 12.1: Paintings on the Wall of New Dukhang

Left down to Centre Fresco

***(2) Rong tsan mar po*[3]**

Height: 1' 10"

Width: 1' 5"

Vahan: Red horse

Mudra: Wrathful, holds small *dhvaja* of five colour small cloth pieces with small mirror called *Dadar* in his left hand. Right hand holds *Sankha.*

Garments: Upper red robe with inner golden; the rest cloths are in red colour.

Offerings down to Centre Fresco Right to Left

(i) Jewel (Norbu)
(ii) Pot (Patra)
(iii) *Cakra* with flower
(iv) *Sankha*

Centre Fresco just above the Tung pa dorje palzang

(3) Dorje Mithukpa:[4]

Colour: Green with black

Mudra & symbols: Left hand holds standing Vajra in *Dhyana* mudra. Right hand is in *Bhumisparsha.*

Garments: Upper and lower limbs are covered by red cloths

Hairs: Tied up like *yogi*

Asana: Dhyana

Crown: Five golden leafed

Right Side of the Dorje Mithuk Pa

(4) Dubs Thabs Rgbya Rtsa Nas Jung Ve Dukar Mo[5]

Crown: Five golden leafed

Height: 1' 10"

Width: 1' 5"

Mudra & symbols: Six arms. Among right hands hold:

(i) *Dharmacakra* near the chest
(ii) Ankusha
(iii) Bow (capa)

Left Hands Hold

(i) Standing vajra near heart

(ii) Demon rope (pasa)

(iii) Arrow (Sara)

Garments: Warlike golden cover.

Red shawl for upper and mixed clothes viz. red, yellow, golden etc. for lower limbs.

Posture: Seated.

Left Side of the Dorje Mithuk Pa

***(5) Green Tara*[6]**

Colour: Green

Crown: Five golden leafed

Asana: Seated

2. Saskya Trizin Nag Wang Kunga Thek Chen Pal bar trinles wang gi gyalpo[7]

Position: Centre fresco

Hat: Conical cap

Colour: White

Garments: Chosgos - Red

Cemse - Golden

Murals & Symbols: Right hand holds vajra near the middle of chest. Left hand holds ball (Ghanta) and rests in the middle of asana.

Height: 3' 1"

Width: 2' 7" (From the bottom of the fresco)

Width: 2' 2" (From the middle of the fresco through chest)

Offerings: Right to Left

(i) Fruits

(ii) *Damru*

(iii) Cakra

(iv) Rice in patra

} These offerings are placed on the small table before the centre fresco.

The following Buddhist dities and Bodhisattvas are depicted in the mandala of the above centre fresco.

Right Down Side of the Centre Fresco

(1) Ngor ludhing khanpo jamyang stanpe nyia[8]

Colour: White

Asana: Seated

Hat: Like Crown

Garments: Chosgos: Red

Camse: Red

Symbols & Mudras: Right hand holds vajra, rests near the middle of chest. Left hand holds *tilbu* (bell), lies on asana.

Offerings Right to Left

(i) Pot
(ii) *Damru*
(iii) Fruits in *lungze*
(iv) bowl

} All these are placed on small table called (*Tsok-tse*).

Centre Fresco Just above the Saskya Trizin Nag Wang Kunga Thyek Chen Pal bar trinles wang gi gyalpo

(2) Chepakmet[9]

Colour: Red

Asana: Dhyana

Mudras & Symbol: Both hands in *Dhyana* mudra with long life pot at the centre of the asana.

Garments: Green shawl for upper; lower mixed colour robe.

Right to the Chepakmet

(3) Tsuktor nampar gyal ma[10]

Colour: White

Posture: Seated

Faces: Three faces; middle white, right golden and left blue.

Eyes: Each face consists three eyes.

Crown: The central face consists three golden leafed, the rest consists one crown each.

Hands: Eight

Symbols and Mudras: Among right hands hold:

(i) Visava vajra of four colour, lies near heart.

(ii) Red jewel (Norbu)

(iii) Arrow

(iv) *Varada* mudra

Left hands Hold:

(i) Demon rope rests near heart

(ii) *Abhaya* mudra

(iii) Bow

(iv) *Dhyana* mudra with standing vajra lies at the midole of asana.

Asana: Dhyana

Garments: Green shawl for Upper; Lower mixed colour robe.

Down Left Side of the Centre Fresco

(4) Dayang Lhamo Yang Chen Ma (Sarasvati):[11]

Colour: White

Crown: Five golden leafed

Mudra and Symbol: Right hand holds a guitar, rests near heart, left hand holds it from the top. The colour of guitar is blue

Garments: Upper inner--light blue

Upper -- Red shawl

Lower--Mixed colour

Ornaments: Golden

Legs: Two, crossed seated

Head: One

Hands: Two

Left to the Chepakmet

(5) Dolkar: White Tara[12]

Face: One

Hands: Two

Legs: Two

Eyes: Seven

She is adored with robes and various ornaments.

3. Snyan gyut gyat tsoi nga dhag tsar chen dorje[13]

Position: Centre Fresco

Colour: Golden

Garments: Hat: Red

Upper part of the body--Red

Lower part of the Body--Red

Symbols and Mudras: Right hand holds vajra, rests near chest. Left hand holds bell (*Ghanta*), rest at the middle of asana.

Asana: Dhyana

Height: 3'

Width: 2' 10" (From base)

Offerings: Lotus (Padma), a symbol of Padmapani, water pot, cakra on flower, Lungze on the flower.

In the mandala of snyan gyut gyat tsoi nga dhag tsar chen dorje the following lamas, deities and Bodhisattvas are depicted.

Right down to the Centre Fresco

(1) Jampal Yang ngos khyen tseiwang poi zhabs[14]

Colour: White

Garments: (Lama Dress) Hat--Red

Upper--Red

Lower--Red

Symbols and Mudras: Right hand holds sword with vajra in varada mudra. Left hand holds bell, rests in the middle of asana and *pothi* on the white lotus flower.

Asana: Dhyana

Left Down to the Centre Fresco

(2) Sang Dhag ngos jon loter wang poi zhabs[15]

Colour: White with pink.

Mudra: Right hand in Dharmacakra. Left hand holds *pothi*, rests in the middle of the asana.

Garments: Hat--Red

Upper--Red

Lower--Red

Heard: One

Hands: Two

Right Up to the Centre Fresco

(3) Khas dup je we tsug gyan naropa[16]

Colour: White with pink

Hairs: Tied like *yogi*

Crown: Single skull

Symbols and Mudras: Right hand holds vajra, rests near chest. Left hand holds skull cup.

Dress: Upper--Blue

Lower--Pink

Lower--Pink

Scraf--Green

Ornaments: Bodhisattva ornaments with green colour.

Asana: Seated on deer skin.

Below the Khas dup je we tsuggyan naropa

(4) Ludub gya tso sang chan nor bui zot[17]

Colour: White with pink

Garments: (Lama Dress) Hat: Red
Upper: Red
Lower: Red
Mudra: Right hand in *Varada* mudra. Left in *Dhyana.*

Hands: Two

Head: One

Left up to the Centre Figure

(5) Dub pa chog gi dhed pon dam ze che[18]

Colour: Pink

Hairs: White

Beard: White

Garments: Upper - white
Lower - white

Mudra: Right hand in *Dharmacakra* mudra. Left hand in Varada.

Below the Duspa Chog gi dhed pon dam ze che

(6) Zab sang zod zin khyen tse wang chug zhabs[19]

Colour: Pink

Garments: (Lama dress) Hat - Red
Upper - Red
Lower - Red

Mudra: Vitarka mudra, holds second finger touches thumb, rests near heart. Left hand holds *pothi,* lies at the middle of asana

Hands: Two

Head: One

Legs: Two

4. Gyal was lung stan ngor chen zhe[20]

Position: Centre fresco

Colour: Golden

Garments: (Lama dress) Hat - Red
Upper - Red
Lower - Red

Mudra: Holds vajra on white lotus on right side, bell on white lotus on left side. *Vajrahumkara* mudra. Buddha supreme and Eternal, wrists crossed at breast.

Asana: Dhyana

Height: 3'

Width: 2' 9" (From the base)

Offerings: White lotus, water pot, *Dharmacakra, Sankha* etc. The following deities and Bodhisattvas are depicted in the mandala of *Gyal was lung stan ngor chen zhe.*

Right up to the Centre Fresco

***(1) Shar Chen Yeshes Gyaltsen zhabs*[21]**

Colour: Pink

Garments: Hat - Red
Upper - Red
Lower - Red

Mudra and symbol: Holds *pothi* by his both hands, lies in the middle of asana.

Head: One

Hands: Two

Legs: Two

Below the shar chen yeshes Gyatsen zhabs

***(2) Mra we nyi ma goram zham pa*[22]**

Colour: Pink

Garments: (Lama dress) Hat - Red
Upper - Red
Lower - Red

Symbols and Mudra: Right hand in *Dharmacakra* mudra. Left hand holds *pothi*, lies in the middle of asana.

Hands: Two

Head: One

Legs: Two

Below the mra we nyima goram zham pa

(3) Khan chen khas dub gyal tsoi zhabs

Colour: Pink

Crown: One golden (Trangle shape)

Garments: (Lama dress) Upper - Red
Lower - Red

Symbols and Mudras: Right hand in varada. Left hand holds jewel (mani) with *Dhyana* mudra.

Left up to the Centre Fresco

(4) Dub pe wang po Buddhasri[24]

Colour: Pink

Garments: (Lama dress) Hat - No (Not weared)
Upper - Red
Lower - Red

Mudra: *Dhyana*

Hands: Two

Legs: Two

Head: One

Below the dub pe wang po Buddhasri

(5) Jamyang Konchog Lung dup zhabs[25]

Colour: Pink

Garments: Hat - Red
Upper - Red
Lower - Red

Symbols and Mudra: Dharmacakra. Right hand holds Khadga with Padma (lotus) flower. Left hand *pothi* with lotus flower.

Below Jamyang Konchog lung dup zhabs

(6) Shar chen lung rtogs gyal tsan zabs[26]

Colour: Pink

Hat: Conical golden

Garments: (Lama dress) Upper - Red

Lower - Red

Mudra: *Dharmacakra.* Right hand holds Khadga with padma. Left hand pothi with lotus flower.

5. Rtse chen kung ga snying poi zhabs[27]

Colour: Golden

Garments: Inner white, Upper red robe and white coat. Lower golden *camse.*

Mudras and Symbol: Right hand varada. Left hand holds white lotus near the breast.

Height: 3' 6"

Width: 2' 8" (From the base).

The following deities and Bodhisattvas are depicted in the mandala.

Right up to the Centre Fresco

(1) Jalus ngos dup sodnam rtse (Sonam tsemo)[28]

Colour: Pink

Garments: Without hat; inner white, red robe with green belt and white coat. Lower golden.

Mudras and Symbol: Dharmacakra

Below Jalus ngos dup sodnam rtse

(2) Saskya Panchen Kungai Tsan[29]

Colour: Pink

Garments: (Lama dress) Hat : Red

Upper: Red

Lower: Red

Mudras and Symbol: Dharmacakra. Right hand holds sword with lotus. Left hand holds pothi with lotus flower.

Asana: Dhyana

Offerings: Lotus flower, water pot, fruits in *lungze.*

Left to the Centre Fresco

(3) Dub Chog drag pa gyaltsen zhabs[30]

Colour: Pink

Garments: Without cap, inner white, upper red robe, white coat, Lower golden camse.

Mudras and Symbol: Right hand holds vajra, rests near breast. Left hand holds bell, lies in the middle of the asana.

Below Dub chog drag pa Gyaltsen zhabs

Phags pa lotos gyaltsen zabs[31]

Colour: Pink

Garments: (Lama dress) Cap - Red

Upper - Red

Lower - Red

Mudras and Symbol: Right hand in *Bhumisparsha.* Left hand holds Chakra in *Dhyana* mudra.

Asana: *Dhyana*

Head: One

Hands: Two

Legs: Two

Offerings: White lotus, water pot, fruits in *lungze.*

6. Sri zhi schi pad me sanphava[32]

Position: Centre fresco

Colour: Golden

Garments: (Lama dress) Hat: Red
Upper - Red
Lower - Red
Inner - Blue

Mudras and Symbol: Holds vajra in right hand, rests near breast. Left hand holds skull cup with *trishul*.

Asana: Lalitasana. Left leg pendant. Other leg in usual position of Buddha-like position of Green Tara, Manjusri etc.

Height: 3' 8"

Width: 3' 3" (From base)

Offerings: White lotus water pot lungze with fruits.

In the mandala the following deities and Bodhisattvas are depicted.

Right up to the Centre Fresco

(1) Gyalwas lung snags phags chog ludub zhabs[33]

Colour: Pink

Garments: Without hat, at the dise of bright light around his head is decorated with eight snakes of different colours

Mudra: Ti-tshap[34]

Asana: Lalitasana. Left leg pendant. Other leg in usual position of Buddha.

Below the Gyalwas lung snags phags chog ludub zhabs

(2) Lta ngan mu stegs tsar chat phags pa lha[35]

Colour: Pink

Garments: Hat - Red
Inner for upper body - Green
Lower - Red

Mudra: Right hand in *Dharmacakra.* Left hand in *Bhumisparsha*

Asana: Latitasana.

Below lta ngan mu stegs tsar chat phags pa lha

***(3) Phas rgol stobs joms chogs kyi lang po gyal*[36]**

Colour: Pink

Garments: (Lama dress) Hat - Red

Upper - Red

Lower - Red

Mudra: Debate, Right hand stretched up. Left hand stretched down to earth. Palm is facing to earth.

***(4) Bum thak dhul wai zot zin yot tan ot*[37]**

Colour: Pink, Garments: Cap-Red, Upper and other cloths red; Mudra: Debate. Right hand stretched plan up. Left-hand palm facing towards earth.

Left up to the Centre Fresco

***(1) Phag yul sing tai srol zet thog met tsan*[38]**

Colour: Pink.

Garments: Cap - Red

Upper body inner - Green

Others - Red.

Mudra: Right hand holds cakra, rests near breast. Left hand holds *pothi,* lies in the middle of asana.

Asana: Lalitasana, Right leg pendant. Left leg in usual position in a Buddha.

Below Phag yul sing tai srol zet thog met tsan

***(2) Chos ngon gya tsoi zot zin yig nyen zabs*[39]**

Colour: White with pink colour

Garments: Hat - Red

Upper inner - Blue

Others - Red

Mudra: Debate. Face stretched near the stomach towards earth. Left hand rests in the middle of asana.

Asana: Right knee raised. Left leg folded inside

Hands: Two

Legs: Two

Head: One

Below chos ngon gya tsoi zot zin yig nyen zabs

(3) Rtsod gyal rig pe wang chug chos kyi dags.

Colour: Pink

Garments: (Lama dress) Hat - Red

Upper - Red

Lower - Red

Mudra: Debate. Right hand stretched palm facing the debator. Left hand in vitarka mudra, index finger touches tip of thumb, palm turned outward.

Hands: Two

Legs: Two

Head: One

Below rstsod gyal rig pe wang chug chos kyi dags

(4) Sri pai zag pa yongs zad sakya odth[41]

Colour: Pink

Garments: Hat - Red

Upper body inner - Blue

Others - Red

Mudra: Debate. Right hand turned back. Left hand palm facing to earth.

Hands: Two

Legs : Two

Hand: One

7. Sakyamuni Buddha[42]

Colour: Golden

Mudra: Right hand in Bhumisparsha. Left hand in meditation.

Garments: Upper - Slightly Red

Lower - Slightly Red

Hands: Two

Legs: Two

Head: One

Height: 3' 8"

Width: 3' 4"

He is flanked by his spiritual sons.

(i) Sariputra on the right, standing, Upper and Lower parts of the body covered by red colour cloths.

(ii) Maudgalyana standing. He also wore the same dress as Sariputra.

Position: Centre fresco.

In his mandala, the following deities and Bodhisattvas are depicted.

Right up to the Centre Fresco

***(1) Miphampa*[43]**

Colour: Golden

Mudra: Dharmacakra

Asana: Bhadrasana; both legs pendant. Position (likely to stand up) of Maitreya.

Garments: (Lama dress) Upper - Red

Lower - Red

Below Miphampa

***(2) De not leg dut kung gao*[44]**

Colour: Pink

Garments: (Lama dress) Upper - Red

Lower - Red

Without Cap

Mudra: Right hand's first, second and third fingers touch the tip of thumb rests near heart. Left hand holds lungze, raised up.

Hands: Two

Leg: Two

Heads: One

Below de not leg dut kung gao

***(3) Leng stan dud dul nyer bas chog*[45]**

Colour: Pink

Garment: All cloths are red, does not wear cap.

Mudra: Right hand facing water pot, placed in front of him, Left hand holds lunze pot.

Hands: Two

Legs: Two

Head: One

Below leng stan dud dul nyer bas chog

***(4) Nyin mor cet pa nag poi zabs*[46]**

Colour: Pink

Garments: Without hat; others red.

Mudra: Right hand in Abhaya. Left hand's palm turned inside rests on asana.

Hands: Two

Legs: Two

Head: One

Left Up to the Centre Fresco

***(1) Gyal chabs chog gyur ot sung tse*[47]**

Colour: Pink

Garments: Without cap, all other cloths are red

Mudra: Right hand varada, all fingers extended downward, palm turned outward. Like mudra of Dolma.

Asana: Lalitasana. One leg pendant. Other is usual position of a Buddha.

Below to Gyal chabs chog gyur ot sung tse

(2) Nog cin dul zat sane cos chen[48]

Colour: Pink

Garments: (Lama dress) Without - Hat

Upper - Red

Lower - Red

Mudra: Left hand in Vitarka, arm bent, all fingers extended upward, except index finger which touches tip of thumb. Palm turned outward. Right hand in varada, charity or gift bestowing; arm pendant, all fingers extended downward, palm turned outward.

Asana: Rajalilasana. Right knee raised. Left leg is in usual position of a Buddha.

Hands: Two

Legs: Two

Head: One

Below Nog cin dul zat sane cos chen

(3) Ta ngan chos zat de ti ka[49]

Colour: Pink

Garments: (Lama dress) Without - Hat

Upper - Red

Lower - Red

Mudra: Left hand in vitarka, Right hand in Bhumisparsha.

Below ta ngan chos zat de ti ka.

(4) Nga gya tul wa legs thong che[50]

Colour: Pink

Garments: Without cap. Red shawl for upper body. Red robe for lower limbs.

Mudra: Debate. Both hands stretched outward, right hand palm rests on the left hand palm, facing upward.

Asana: Raised right knee up.

Hands: Two

Legs: Two

Head: One

Wall Paintings on the left side wall of the Main Throne

On this wall I saw maximum number of windows. The murals are depicted on the wall above the windows. An elaborate description is stated below.

8. *Bara da za ser can la*[51]

Mudra: Dhyana

Hands: Two

Head: One

Garments: (Lama dress) Upper - Red

Lower - Red

9. *Phags pe nas tan ser byu*[52]

Mudra: Vitarka; holds rosary (*mala*) in right hand.

Hands: Two

Head: One

Legs: Two

Asana: Lalitasana

10. Phags pe nastan zang po ni[53]

Mudra: Right hand Vitarka, Left hand in Dhyana.

Hands: Two

Head: One

Legs: Two

11. Nastan Dorje moi bu[54]

Mudra: Right hand in Vitarka mudra. Left hand in Varada with stick and cloth.

Hands: Two

Head: One

Legs: Two

12. Phags pe nastan dus dan nyi[55]

Mudra: Right hand Vitarka, Left hand in Varada.

Hands: Two

Legs: Two

Head: One

13. Phags pe nastan Nags na nas[56]

Mudra: Right hand placed near Asana. Left hand holds stick with cloth on its top.

Asana: Folded both his legs.

Hands: Two

Legs: Two

Head: One.

14. Phags pe nas tan mi phampa[57]

Mudra: Dhyana

Asana: Dhyana

Garments: To put shawl upto head.

Head: One

Hands: Two

Legs: Two

15. Phags pe nas tan yan lak zung[58]

Mudra: Right hand holds stick with cloth near chest. Left hand holds stick, palm turned up.

16. Phags pe ge nyen Dhrmta[59]

This fresco is painted in between Sl. No. 12 and 13.

Mudra: Holds Ladakhi pungpa (pot) near heart in his right hand. Left hand holds stick.

Asana: Seated on lion's bluish skin.

Hairs: Tied like *yogi.*

17. Sa-tug stok pa phul gyur nas sta ngan ri zik birupa[60]

Position: Centre Fresco

Colour: Brownish

Mudra: Te-thabs

Asana: Crossed legs

Garments: Upper - No cloths

Lower - Red robe.

Put scarf from right shoulder to left shoulder.

Ornaments: Flower with bones garland.

Crown: Five leafed with bones.

Symbols: Right side on pungpa bone cup. Left side blue pungpa.

In the mandala of sa-tug-stok-pa-phul-gyur-nas sta ngan ri-zik-birupa the following deities and Bodhisattvas are depicted.

Right up to the Centre Fresco

(1) Zag mo do de ton zig sin chod dal yak ston sangyas pal

Mudra: Right hand in vitarka. Left hand in Dhyana mudra with *cakra.*

Hands: Two

Head: One

Legs: Two

Garments: (Lama dress) Hat - Red

Upper - Red

Lower - Red

Right down to the Centre Fresco

(2) Do ngag gons ton tal khaspa panchen sakya chog dan jabs[62]

Mudra: Right hand in vitarka. Left hand holds *pothi,* rests in the middle of asana.

Left up to the Centre Fresco

(3) Dek sum chat la mi zik pe se za kun zik rongs ton ze[63]

Mudra: Ti-thabs. Right hand holds cakra with white lotus. Left hand holds water pot with white lotus.

Garments: (Lama dress) Hat - Red
Upper - Red
Lower - Red

Left down to Centre Fresco

(4) Rab zam gyud de mar vang zong pa kung ga namgyal chog[64]

Mudra: *Ti-thabs.* Right hand holds standing vajra with lotus. Left hand holds *tilbu* with lotus flower.

Dress: (Lama dress) Hat - Red
Upper - Red
Lower - Red

Head: One

Hands: Two

Legs: Two

18. Four Frescos Together

(1) Right up: Kadam stan pe mig cet Atisa[65]

Mudra: Left and Right hand together hold cakra.

Garments: Hat - Red
Upper body inner - Light blue
Others - Red cloths

Asana: Dhyana

(2) Right Down Side: Zha ser stan pe srog shing lozang daks[66]

Mudra: Right hand holds sword with white lotus. Left hand holds *pothi* with white Padma.

Hands: Two

Head: One

Legs: Two

Asana: Dhyana

(3) Left up: Dup pe Gyal tsen dengs khas mi la ze[67]

Garments: Without hat. Upper and lower garments are white.

Mudra: Right hand hide near the ear. Left hand holds skull cup, rests in the middle of asana.

Asana: Right leg knee raised. Seated on deer skin.

Left down Side

(4) Theg pa chog gi sing ta long chen chog[68]

Mudra: Both hands are in Bhumisparsha. Right hand holds sword with white lotus. Left hand holds *pothi* with white lotus.

Garments: (Lama dress) Hat - Red

Upper - Red

Lower - Red

19. Phags pe nas tan Bakula[69]

20. Phags pe nas tan da can zin: Crown: Five leafed.[70]

21. Phags pe nas tan lam tan stan[71]

Mudra: Meditation

Hands: Two

Legs: Two

Head: One

22. Bara da za sod nyuoms len[72]

Mudra: Right hand holds *pothi.* Left hand holds lungze.

Hands: Two

Head: One

Legs: Two

23. Phas pe nas tan lams tan ni[73]

Mudra: Right hand in Vitarka mudra. Left hand holds *pothi.*

Hands: Two

Legs: Two

Head: One

24. Phagspe Nastan lu yi de[74]

Mudra: Right hand holds pot. Left hand holds *Kharsil.*

Hands: Two

Head: One

Legs: Two

25. Phags pe nastan sbet chet ni[75]

Mudra: Both hands hold pothi in the middle.

Hands: Two

Head: One

Legs: Two

26. Phags pe nastan mi chet pa[76]

Mudra: Holds stupa. Both hands in offering position.

Hands: Two

Head: One

Legs: Two

27. Sangyas khor ces can dangs pe zor dan gyal po ha sang ze[77]

This mural is depicted below in between Sl. No. 18 and 19.

Garments: (Lama dress) Coat - Red

Lower - Red

Mudra: Right hand holds fruit, rests near chest. Left hand holds gold garland.

Hands: Two

Legs: Two

Head: One

28. Not sjin ter dak gyal sten nam tos sras[78]

This mural is depicted below the fresco Sl. No. 22.

Vahan: Tibetan white lion

Crown: Golden three leafed

Garments: Warlike dress

Hands: Two

Legs: Two

Head: One

Along the Door

29. Kundarik nampar nangzat[79]

Position: Centre fresco

Colour: White

Faces: Four, Central face consists five leafed crown. Other faces have singe crown.

Mudra: Dhyana

Asana: Dhyana

Height: 3' 2"

Width: 2' 7" (From base)

Offerings: Jewel

The following deities and Bodhisattvas are depicted in the mandala.

Right up to the Centre Fresco

(1) Lo Chen Rin chen zang po[80]

Mudra: Meditation

Asana: Meditation

Hat - Red

Sky blue inner for. Other cloths are red.

Below Lo Chen Rin Chen Zang Po

(2) Tadin (Hagriva)[87]

Mudra: Wrathful form.

Faces: Three. Middle face has five skulls crown. The rest have single skull crown.

Colour: Centre face - Red

Right face - Green

Left face - White

Body Colour - Red with red flames

Hands: Six

Right hands hold:

(i) Vajra, rests near heart

(ii) Trishul with three skulls

(iii) Sword.

Left hands hold:

(i) Index finger up

(ii) Single trishul

(iii) Demon rope.

Ornaments: Snake and other gold ornaments of *Dharmapala*.

Asana: Standing on snake

Below the Hagriva

***(3) Kyung tha*[82]**

Mudra: Wrathful. Right hand Abhaya. Right hand in Vitarka, rest near chest.

Hair: Golden colour flying hairs, Jewel in the middle.

Crown: Mahe

Eyes: Three

Face: Bird

Body: Upper red human with wings. Lower white eagle.

Left up of the Centre Fresco

***(4) Singe da*[83]**

Body: White colour

Crown: Five golden leafed

Garments: Left shoulders: Deer skin. Right shoulder: Red shawl Lower part of the body: Orange and Red cloths.

Mudra: Right hand - Bhumisparsha

Left hand - Rests on asana

Asana: Lalitasana; one leg pendent . Other leg in usual position of Buddha.

Symbols and Mudra: Khadga with skull and lotus flower in left hand.

Right hand holds Trishul with Snake.

(5) Singdong ma: Below the singe da[84]

Mudra: Wrathful. Left hand holds skull cup, rests near heart and three skulls trishul. Right hand holds Kartika of blue colour.

Colour: Green

Garments: Blue shawl for upper part of the body. Lower - Tiger-skin.

Ornaments: Garland of human skulls and gold garlands.

Eyes: Three

Head: White lion

Hair: Golden flying hairs.

Asana: Standing on human body.

Below Singdongma

(6) Zam-nak[85]

Body: Golden

Mudra: Wrathful, standing on lady corpse. Right hand holds skull cup, rests near heart. Left hand holds magoose, lies near stomach.

Eyes: Three

The fresco is depicted with the mandala of red flames.

30. Gonkar

Colour: White

Hands: Six. Among left hands hold:

(i) Jewel, pungpa in skull cup, rests near the stomach
(ii) Trishul
(iii) Ankusha

Right hands hold:

(i) Jewel rests near the chest
(ii) Kartika
(iii) White *damaru*

Crown: Five golden leafed with mani (Jewel)

Eyes: Three

Ornaments: Dharmapala ornaments with gold garlands.

Garments: Green shawl for upper part of the body. Lower part of body has orange, golden and red robe.

Mudra: Standing on human corpse: Who has elephant head and in left hand holds magoose. Right hand holds two radish.

Height: 4' 6"

Width: 3' 4"

In the mandala the following deities and Bodhisattvas are depicted.

Left up to the Centre Fresco

(1) Zamser[87]

Colour: Golden

Asana: Seated. Lalitasana. One leg pendant other in usual position of a Buddha. Sankara lies below right leg.

Mudra: Right hand holds fruit. Left holds magoose, who is omiting jewels.

Crown: Golden

Garments: Blue shawl for upper part of the body. Orange on red robe for lower part of the body.

Ornament: Flower garlands

Below Zam ser

(2) Zam mar (Yab-yum)[88]

Colour: Red

Yab: Five golden crowns. Three eyes. Right hand holds jewel (mani) and left holds magoose, who is omiting jewels. Wear green shawl on upper part of the body while red robe for lower part.

Yum: Five leafed crowns. Two eyes. Light red body colour facing to yab. Blue with green scarf for upper part of the body. Light green robe for lower part. Left hand holds skull and right hand holds mani (jewel).

Right up to Centre Fresco

(3) Zam kar[89]

Body Colour: White

Crown: Five golden leafed

Eyes: Three

Hairs: Red with white

Vahana: Green dragon, who holds red jewel.

Mudra: Right hand holds trishul (trident) of human skull. Left hand holds danda, rests at waist.

Garments: Green blue shawl for upper part of the body. Orange on red robe for lower part.

Ornaments: Golden Bodhisathva ornaments.

Asana: One leg pendant. Other in usual position of Buddha.

Below Zam kar

(4) Zam lzang in yeb-yum form[90] ***Yab:***

Crown: Five golden leafed

Eyes: Two

Face: One green

Body: Green

Mudra: Right hand holds fruit, rests on right knee. Left hand holds magoose, rests near-heel.

Garments: Green scarf for upper part of the body. Lower part has orange colour on red robe.

Yum: Body: Bluish

Mudra: Yab in Lalitasana. Right leg rests on *sankha.*

Frescos on the Wall above the Door, Rig sum gonpo From Right hand to Left

(a) Manjusri (Jamyang)[91]

Hands: Four

Colour: Golden

Crown: Five golden leafed

Mudra: Right hand holds sword and arrow. Left hand holds bow and white lotus flower with *pothi.*

Garments: Blue shawl for upper part of the body. Lower part has red robe.

Asana: Dhyana

(b) Zung po dul cet[92]

Mudra: Wrathful, with flames, hairs fly like flames of golden colour

Crown: Five skulls

Eyes: Three

Colour: Blue black

Ornaments: Garlands of human skull with snakes and bones.

Hands: Four. Right hand holds vajra. Left hand holds Demon rope. The other two holds in vajra phat mudra.

Vahana: Standing on human body who has three eyes, golden hairs, four hands. Right hands hold- (i) Kartika (ii) Red damaru. Left hands hold- (i) skull cup, (ii) Trishul.

Garments: Blue shawl for upper part of the body. Tiger skin for lower part. The face of tiger facing towards earth.

(c) Avalokitesvara[93]

Hands: Four. Right hand holds mala. Left hand holds Lotus flower. The remaining two hands are put together in Namaskar mudra with mani (jewel).

Crown: Five golden leafed

Body: White colour

Cloth: Green shawl for upper part of the body. Red robe for lower part of the body.

To sum up, I would say this Dukhang has frescos of 16th Arhats and various other Bodhisattvas paintings according to Sakya order of Mahayana Buddhism. Besides four lokpalas are depicted outside of the walls viz. (i) 'aphags kyes po[94] (ii) yul 'akhor srung[95] (iii) sbyanmig bzạng[96] (iv) rnamthos sras.[97]

NOTES AND REFERENCES

1. Tung pa dorje palzang: He was a Sakya Lama, who came to Ladakh during 15th century A.D.
2. Rong tsan kar po: Probably he may be a minor mountain deity.
3. Rong tsan mar po: Probably he may be a minor mountain deity.
4. Dorje Mithukpa: Tib. rdo-rje mi-hkhrugs-pa an alternate spelling of Mi-pskyrd-pa or Skt Aksobhya.
5. Dubs thabs rgbya rpsa nas jung ve dukar mo: He is the deity of Mahayana of Tantric tradition.
6. Green Tara: Tib. sgrol lma ljang. Pron. Dolma Jang-gu or "green savioress" is probably the form of the incarnate in Wencheng, the Chinese wife of king Songtsen Gompo. She is green, sits in the royal posture on the moon disc and lotus flower, her right leg extended, with its foot resting on a small lotus blossom. Face: One, calm; Hands Two, both hold two blue lotus flowers of compassion. Legs-two. Ornaments: Five leafed crown, earring, tight necklace, armlet, a wrap for the lower body and one for the upper, a garland to the thigh and one to the navel, a girdle and sash. Vahana--Lotus throne. She is usually seen seated with the right leg hanging down, in green colour, in peaceable manifestation, and with a dark blue lotus bud as a symbol. Cf. Finegan, Jack: *Tibet: A Dreamt of Image*, Tibet House and Wiley Eastern Ltd., New Delhi. 1986: 136.

7. Saskya Trizin Nag Wang Kunga Thek chen Pal bar trinles wang gi gyalpo: He is the Sakya lama of Sakya tradition of Mahayana Buddhism.
8. Ngor ludhing khanpo jamyang stanpe nyia: He is the head lama of Sakya tradition.
9. Chepakmet: Tib, Ts'e dpag-med, Tshe-dpag-med, che-dpag-med, Tshe-dpag-med-lha dgu, Phon. Eng. Tsepame. "Dispenser of long life." The Bodhisattva of longevity who is invoked for long life, health and happiness. He is depicted in the following way. Face: One, Arms: Two, in dhyana mudra, holding an vase with the elixir of life; a golden vase containing the nectar of immortality and a spring of the myrobalan plant. Ornaments: Five leafed crown ear ring, tight necklace, armlet, wristlet, bracelet, anklet, a wrap for the lower body and one for the upper, a garland to the thigh and one to the navel, a girdle and a sash. Colour: Red. companion-White Tara and Vijaya. Cf. Bunce, Fredrick W.: *An Encyclopaedia of Buddhist Deities, Demigods, Godlings, Saints and Demons,* Vol. I, D.K. Printworld Ltd., New Delhi, 1994: 13.
10. Tsukhor nampar gyal ma: She is the yidam under Tantric Buddhist tradition.
11. Dayang Lhamo yang chen ma (Sarasvati): She is known as the female deity of knowledge, was born from the face of Brahma.
12. Dolkar (White Tara): She is compassion's motherly form. In her "Ordinary" white form she is represented by Astamahabhya Tara and Mrityuvancana Tara. She sits in the full lotus posture on moon and sun discs upon lotus flower. Face: One, calm. Hands: Two, holds a stem of blue lotus of compassion in her hand and right hand is in varada mudra. Legs: Two Ornaments: Five leafed crown, earring, tight necklace, armlet, wrislet, bracelet, anklet, a wrap for the lower body and one for the upper, a garland to the thigh and one to the navel, a girdle and a sash. Vahana: Lotus throne. She is recognised by her seven eyes; three in her face, two in the palms of her hands, and two in the soles of her feet. Cf. Bunce, Fredrick W., *op. cit.,* 542-'43.
13. Snyan gyut gyat tsoi nga dhag tsar chen dorje: He is the deity of Tantric tradition of Mahayana.
14. Jampal yang ngos khyen tseiwang poi zhabs: He is the lama of Nying ma pa tradition of Mahayana Buddhism.
15. Sang dhag ngos jon loter wang poi zhabs: He is the great translator, translated Sanskrit Buddhist texts into Tibetan language.

16. Khas dup je we tsug gyan naropa: He is the great tantric and disciple of Tilopa.
17. Ludub gya tso sang chan nor bui zot: He is lama of Nying ma pa tradition.
18. Dub pa chog gi dhed pon dam ze che: He is a great Dub pa king and Siddha of Ka'gyud tradition.
19. Zab sang zod zin khyen tse wang chug zabs. He is a tantric lama.
20. Gyal was lung stan ngor chen zhe: He is a great tantric lama.
21. Shar chen yeshes Gyaltsen zhabs. He is a great tantric lama.
22. Mra we nyi ma goram zham pa: He is a great Sa-kya lama of Mahayana Buddhism.
23. Khan chen khas dub gyal tsoi zhabs: He is a great Sa-kya lama of Mahayana tradition.
24. Dub pa wang .po Buddhasri: He is a great tantric lama.
25. Jamyang konchog lung dup zhabs: He is a great Sakya lama of Mahayana tradition.
26. Shar chen lung rtogs gyal tsan zabs: He is a great Sakya lama of Mahayana Buddhism.
27. Rtse chen kung ga snying poi zhabs: He is a great Sakya lama of Mahayana Buddhism.
28. Jalus ngos dup sodnam rtse (Sonam tsemo): He is a great Sakya lama of Mahayana Buddhism.
29. Saskya Panchen Kungai tsan: He is a great Sakya lama of Mahayana Buddhism.
30. Dub chog drag pa gyaltsen zhabs: He is a great tantric lama of Mahayana.
31. Phags pa lotos gyaltsen zabs: He is a great Sakya lama of Mahayana Buddhism.
32. Sri zhi schi pad me sanphava: He is a tantric lama of Mahayana Buddhism.
33. Gyalwas lung snags phags chog ludub zhabs. Probably he may be Nagarjuna, a great Indian Acharya.
34. Ti-tshap: A kind of Mudra of the concern deity /Bodhisattva.
35. Lta ngan mu stegs tsar chat phags pa lha: He is a great Indian Buddhist scholar.
36. Phas rgol stobs jams chogs kyi lang po gyal: He is great Indian Buddhist scholar.
37. Bum thak dhul wai zot zin yon tan ot: He is a great Indian Buddhist scholar.

38. Phag yul sing tai srol zet thog met tsan: He was the son of king later became lama of Buddhist tradition and well known scholar of Buddhism.
39. Chos ngon gya tsoi zot zin yig nyen zabs: He is a Indian Buddhist scholar of Nalanda a Buddhist University in India.
40. Rtsord gyal rig pe wang chug chos kyi dags pa: He is a Indian Buddhist scholar of Nalanda a Buddhist University in India.
41. Sri pai zag pa yongs zad sakya odth: He is a Indian Buddhist scholar of Nalanda a Buddhist University.
42. Sakyamuni Buddha: After attaining enlightenment at Bodhgaya. Buddha turned the three wheels of Dharma in three different places viz. Varanasi, Gridrakuta and Vaisali. Besides, he went to Tusita loka and preached gods and goddess along his mother. He turned the wheel of Tantra at Sri Dhanyakuta by menifesting himself into lord vajradhara. The essence of his teachings is known Pratiyasamutpada. At the age of eighty he got Mahaparinirvana in Kushinagar. Hindu worship him as ninth avatar of Vishnu.
43. Miphampa: He is the lama of Sakya tradition of Mahayana Buddhism.
44. De not leg dut kung gao : He is Arya Anada.
45. Leng stan dud dul nyer bas chog: He is a lama of Mahayana tradition.
46. Nyin mor cet pa nag poi zebs: He is a Sakya lama of Mahayana Buddhism.
47. Gyal chabs chog gyur ot sung tse: He is a tantric lama of Mahayana tradition.
48. Nog cin dul zat sane cos chen: He is a lama of Mahayana Buddhism.
49. Ta ngan chos zat de tika: Protector of Dharma.
50. Nga gya tul wa legs thong che: Protector of Dharma.
51. Bara da za ser can la: One of the Arhat in a group of sixteen arhats (Tib. gna brtan, Pron. nepten).
52. Phags pe nas tan ser byu: One of the of sixteen Arhats and is believed to have been entrusted by Sakyamuni Buddha.
53. Phags pe nas tan zang po ni: One of the Arhat entrusted by Sakyamuni Buddha with the continuing test of protecting the Buddha doctrine.
54. Nastan Dorje moi bu: One of the sixteen Arhats who were entrusted by Sakyamuni Buddha for protecting his doctrine.

55. Phags pe nas tan dus dan nyi: One the Arhat who was entrusted to protect the Buddha doctrine.
56. Phags pe nas ten nags na nas: One of the Arhat among sixteen who were entrusted to protect the Buddha doctrine.
57. Phags pe nas ten mi phampa: One of the sixteen Arhats who have been entrusted to protect the Buddha doctrine.
58. Phags pe nas ten yan lak zung: One of the Arhat who has been entrusted to protect the Buddha doctrine for the welfare of human beings.
59. Phags pe ge nyen Dhrmata: Arhat.
60. Sa tug stok pa phul gyur nas sta ngan ri zik birupa: One of the Arhats who was entrusted to protect the Budha doctrine for the welfare of human beings.
61. Zag mo do de ton zig sin chod dal yak ston sangyas pal. One of the Arhats who has been entrusted to protect the Buddha doctrine for the welfare of human beings.
62. Do ngag gons ton tal khaspa panchen sakya chog dan jobs: Sakya lama of Mahayana Buddhism.
63. Dek sum chat la mi zik pe se za kum zik rongs ton ze: A great Sakya lama of Mahayana Buddhism sometimes called Tibetan Buddhism.
64. Rab zam gyud de mar vang zong pa kung ga namgyal chog: A great Sakya lama of Mahayana sect.
65. Kadam stan pe mig cet Atisa: He is one of the eighty-four mahasiddhas, saints and miracle doers, sometimes known as the Eighty-four great sorcerers. They are the great tantrics of Mahayanism, the mahagurus. Cf. Bunce, Fredrick W.: *An Encyclopaedia of Buddhist Deities...* Vol. I, D.K. Printworld, New Delhi, 1994: 34.
66. Zha ser stan pe srog shing lozang daks: He is Tsongkhapa, the founder of Geluk pa order and Ganden monastery in Tibet in 1407 Cf. Finegan, Jack: *'Tibet: A Dreamt of Image,* Tibet House, 1986: 101.
67. Dup pe Gyal tsen dengs khas mi la ze: He is a great Drug pa (Duk-pa) lama of Mahayana Buddhism.
68. Theg pa chog gi sing ta long chen chog: He is a great scholar lama of Nying ma pa.
69. Phags pe nas tan Bakula: Arhat Bakula is one of the sixteen Arhats. It is believed that he has been entrusted by Sakyamuni Buddha to protect his doctrine.

70. Phags pe nas tan da can zin: He is an Arhat, who has been entrusted by Sakyamuni Buddha to protect his doctrine.
71. Phags pe nas tan lam tan stan: He is an Arhat, has been entrusted by Sakyamuni Buddha to protect his doctrine.
72. Bara da za sod nyuoms len: He is an Arhat among sixteen famous Arhats, who have been entrusted by Sakyamuni Buddha.
73. Phags pe nas tan lams tan ni: He is one among sixteen famous Arhats who have been entrusted by Sakyamuni Buddha.
74. Phags pe nas tan lu yi de: He is an Arhat among sixteen famous Arhats.
75. Phags pe nas tan sbet chet ni: He is one among the sixteen Arhats who have been entrusted by Sakyamuni Buddha to protect his doctrine.
76. Phags pa nas tan mi chet pa: He is one of sixteen famous arhats who have been entrusted by Sakyamuni Buddha.
77. Sangyas Khor ces can dangs pe zor dan gyal po ha sang ze: Hasang or H Vasang. He was the rich man who helped Arhats for the propogation of Buddhism.
78. Not sjin ter dak gyal tsen nam tos sras: He is Nam tos sras or lokpala in Sanskrit equivalent Kubera, guardian of the North and king of Yakshas.
79. Kundrik nampar nangzat: Verocana (or Vairocana). A Dhyani Buddha whose dominion in the centre of the world. His recognition symbol is the wheel. Winter is the season.
80. Lo chen Rin chen gang po: He is a great translator.
81. Tandin (Hagriva): Tib. rta - mgrin rta - mgrin - rgyal - pa phon. Eng. Tamdin, in Sanskrit equivalent to aka Arya - Hayagriva krodha yamari "The horse-necked one." A krodhadevatas and dharmapala and a protective deity who keeps away demons. He is a wrathful emanation of Avalokitesvara and functions as both powerful protector who destroys evil spirits and a deity in tantric practice. Cf. Bunce, Fredric W.: *An Encyclopaedia of Buddhist Deities,* Vol. I., D.K. Printworld Ltd., New Delhi, 1994: 202.
82. Kyung tha: He is sungma (Dharma Protector).
83. Singe da: Tib. Senge-sgra Skt. Simhanada, "The lord with the vice of a lion." A non-tantric form of Dhyani Bodhisattva Avalokitesvara who is prayed to a care of leprosy.
84. Singdong ma (or Seng dong Tib. seng gdong): She is a lhamo depicted in the mandala of Paldan Lhamo, Sridevi; a guardian deity and the main protector of Gelukpa tradition of Mahayana.

85. Zam nak: Sungma (Dharma Protector).
86. Gonkar: A form of Mahakala. He is depicted in the following way: Face: One, fierce, three eyes. Arms: Six: Holding wish fulfilling jewel (yid-bzhin-nor-bu), skull-cup (kapala, thod-pa), Ritual chopper (karttrika, grig-gug), Human skull - drum, goad/ hook, Trident. Legs: Two-stands on two elephants, colour: white, Vahana -Two elephants. He is depicted in Dukhang Kirmo Cf. Bunce, Fredrick W.: *An Encyclopaedia of Buddhist Deities,* Vol. I, D.K. Printworld, New Delhi; 1994: 179 and 307.
87. Zamser: He is sungma (Dharma Protector).
88. Zam-mar (yab-yun): He is yidam in Sanskrit equivalent Ishtadeva, tutelary or protective deity depending upon the concern sect of the monastery.
89. Zam kar: He is yidam; Skt. Ishtadeva; tutelary or protective deity.
90. Zam lzang (yab-yun): Yidam, Skt. Ishtadeva; tutelary or protective deity.
91. Manjusri. Tob. 'Jam dhyangs, "Charming Splendor," and is shown in yellow, white, red, blue and black forms; beautifully handsome young mahabodhisattva and bodhisattva and god of wisdom, science and agriculture., Cf. Bunce, Fredrick W., *op. cit.,* 331.
92. Zung po dul cet: Yidam; in Sanskrit language equivalent Ishtadeva, tutelary or personal protective deity.
93. Avalokitesvara: Tib. Chenrezi. He has many forms. A Mahabodhisattva and one of the most popular Bodhisattvas in the world of Buddhism. The Fourth Dhyani Bodhisattva, the creator and ruler of the present age, an emanation of Dhyani Buddha Amitabha, who was born from shining white ray of light which sprang from meditation. He can be identified with one face and four hands. Cf. Bunce, Fredrick W., *op. cit.,* 36.
94. 'Aphags kyes po: In Sanskrit equivalent to virudhaka. He is the king of the South, is blue in colour and carries a sword and scabbard, as a lord and master over the kumbhandas, giant, demons and gnomens, he is depicted as one face, angry; two arms; richly dressed; vahana-elephant. He is depicted with sword. Cf. Batchelor, Stephen: *The Tibet Guide,* Wisdom Pub., London, 1987: 426.
95. Yul 'akhor srung: In Sanskrit equivalent to Dhritarashtra. He is the guardian king of the east, white in colour and plays a flute as he rules the realm that lives on melodious music. He is one of

the Lokpalas known as 'place guardinan' or protective deity of east direction. Cf. Finegan, Jack: *Tibet: A Dreamt of Image,* Tibet House, New Delhi, 1986: 134 and Batchelor, Stephen: *'The Tibet Guide',* Wisdom Publication, London, 1987: 426.

96. Sbyan mig bzang: In Sanskrit equivalent to Virupaksha. He is one of the Lokpalas (Tib. Gyalchen dezhi or Gyaltsen zee). There are four guardians of the four cardinal points, called four cardinal kings. They are normally shown as warriors, wearing costs of nail, boots, and headdress or crown, and distinguished by their different colours. The virupaksha is in red colour and the guardian king of west. He holds a small stupa in his right hand and a snake in his left. Cf. Finegan, Jack: *Tibet: A Dreamt of Image, op.cit.:* 134 and Batchelor, Stephen:' *The Tibet Guide, op.cit.:* 426.

97. rnam thos sras: Skt. Vaishravana, also known as Kubera and Jambhala. He is the guardian king of the north and Buddhist god of wealth; Vahana: White lion, golden yellow in colour, he has a large rounded body, Hands: Two-holds silk banner of victory in his right hand, holds a mongoose that vomits jewels in his left hand. The mongoos keep pouring gems out of its mouth and with a banner in his hand causing showers of wealth to fall by his merely shaking of it. Cf. Finegan, Jack: *'Tibet: A Dreamt of Image',* Tibet House, New Delhi, 1986: 134 and Batchelor, Stephen: *'The Tibet Guide,'* Wisdom Pub., London; 1987: 426.

13

Statues in New Dukhang (Dukhang Soma)

The Dukhang Soma or new Dukhang has one big statue of Sakyamuni Buddha (Fig. 13.1).

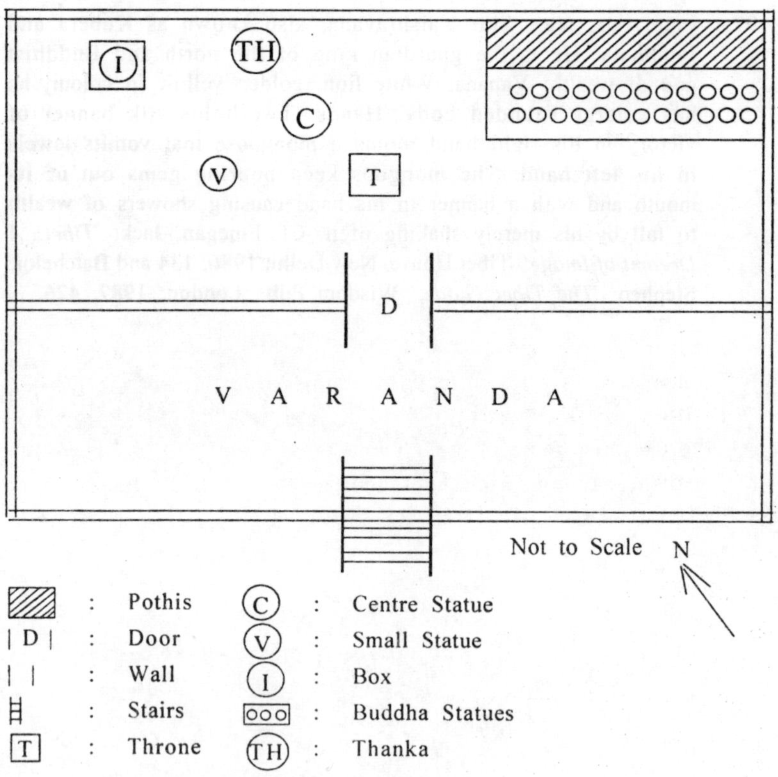

Fig. 13.1: Statues in New Dukhang

(C) The New Dukhang has one central statue of Sakyamuni Buddha. Here follows its measurements:

Height: 5" 4"

Width: 2'

Sakyamuni statue is with his two main disciples viz. Sariputta and Maudgalyayana. In Tibetan language it is spelled as Shakya Tubpa Pron. Tubpa. The Enlightened one or "The Awakened one." Historically known as Gautama Buddha. In 6th Century B.C. Buddha descended to the world to show the right path to the fortunate beings by taking birth in a royal family in Lumbini. Later he married Yasodhara who gave birth to a son Rahula. As took birth in this world Buddha did not like worldly pleasure, instead he felt happiness by showing the right path to all beings, so that they may attain freedom from the cycle of existence. He practiced Bodhisattva activities for countless aeons to attain perfect enlightenment.[1]

(V) ***Vajrapani:*** A small statue. In Tibetan language Pron. Phyag dor, phyag na rdo rje tho drug pa. He is the Bodhisattva of energy and power. During peaceful aspect, he is expressed as a blue Bodhisattva holding a lotus. Face: One, fierce, three eyes, flame- like hair. Arms-Two, holds vajra in his right hand and left hand is placed before his heart. Legs- Two. Ornaments - Five leafed crown, earring, tight necklace, armlet, wristlet, bracelet, anklet, a lion skin wrap for the lower body, a garland to the thigh and one to the navel, a girdle. Colour-Dark blue. Vahana - lotus throne. Vajrapani is the emanation and spiritual son of the Dhyani Buddha Aksobhya. He is also the protector of Nagas and may assume a Garuda form in this role. When appearing with the Buddha he is always on the left side of the Buddha. He is also considered by the Northern Buddhists as one of the eight Dhyani Bodhisattvas. The various forms of Vajrapani are: Achala - Vajrapani, Acharya Vajrapani, Alpacanda Vajrapani,

Amoghatrana Vajrapani, Badidar, Bhutadamara Anuttara Vajrapani, Bhuytadamara Vajrapani, Bhutadamara Vajrapani, Chanda Vajrapani, Garudayata Vajrapani, hgro bzan lugs rilambaradhara Vajrapani, Jagaddama Vajrapani, Khra Thogs Canda Vajrapani, Krodha Vajrapani, Kutagara Vajrapani, Lahanadi Vajrapani, Mahachakra Vajrapani, Mahachakra Vajrapani, Buddha, Nava Bhutadamara Vajrapani, Ne-sras bragyad kyi nan chen phyag na rje ljan khu, Niladanda Vajrapani, Nilambaradhara, Nilambaradhara Vajrapani, Nila Vajrapani, Rakta Alpachanda Vajrapani, Ras chun lugs bsrun bahi mkhar canda maharosana Vajrapani, Raudra Vajrapani, Santa Vajrapani, Sa-skya-lugs Vajrapani, Sri-vcarya Vajrapani, Sutra Krama Vajrapani, Syama Vajrapani, Vcarya, Vcarya Vajrapani.[2]

(T) Throne for the head lama of Matho monastery. The measurements of this throne is as follows:

Height: 9' 5"

Width: 4' 8"

The throne is decorated by Ladakhi carving of dragon and flowers etc.

(I) Instruments box painted with Tashi stag gyat[3] and flowers.

(ooo) 101 small Buddha statues in glass frame almirah

(***) 118 pothis including two old pothis.

(TH) Sashen Kunga Nying po (Tib. Sa chen kun dga' snying po)

Position: Centre figure of the Thanka. The following figures in the mandala

Up right: snangsritzilnon chog (Padmasambhava)

Up left: Vajradhara

Colour: Dark green

Offering: Lotus flower with mirror, *shankha*, fruits, two *silyan* on the flower and at the bottom *Norbu*

Frame:	Height:	6' 9"
	Width:	4' 2"
Painting:	Width:	2' 6"
	Height:	3' 4"
Style:	Pasted cloth pieces according to figures.	

The new Dukhang is also called as Jamyang Chokhang. It was constructed in 1970 under the direction of Dr. Jamyang Gyaltsan who was then the head of Cultural and Welfare Society, Mangtro (Matho) Monastery, Leh. This Dukhang has eight pillars and in the middle has one big throne for Skyabgon Thichen Dorje chang chenpo (Tib. skyabs - mgon khri chen rdo - rje 'achang chen po). Besides, chagzot Rgzin Hanu (Tib. Phyad mdzod rig 'adzin ha nu) and Lama Tsering (Tib. dge tse ring rdo-rje) also contributed their valuable support during the construction of the said Dukhang. Unfortunately major cracks were noticed after the construction of the same. Therefore, on the advice of civil engineer it was renovated this in 2007 during summer season.

NOTES AND REFERENCES

1. Lobzang Tsewang: *Sakyamuni: An Exhibition of Rare Thankas,* CIBS, Leh Ladakh, 2001: 20.
2. Bunce, Fredric W.: *An Encyclopaedia of Buddhist Demigods, Godlings, Saints, and Demons,* Vol. I, D.K. Print World Pvt. Ltd., New Delhi, 1994: 397 and Bachelor Stephen: *'The Tibet Guide,'* Wisdom Pub., London, 1987: 403-'04.
3. Tashi stag gyat: These are also called white parasol, keep away the heat of evil desires; two fishes symbols of happiness and utility; seashell, symbol of blessedness of turning to the right; lotus, pledge of salvation and symbol of divine origin; vase, treasury of all desires; standard (victorious banner) erected on summit of Mount Meru, centre of Buddhist Universe; wheel, leads to perfection, its right spokes symbolizing the eight fold path: endless knot, mystic diagram symbol of the endless cycle of rebirths. Cf. Antoinette K. Gordon: *The Iconography of Tibetan Lamaism.* Munshiram Manoharlal, Publishers Pvt. Ltd.. Originally Pub. 1914; Reprinted 1998: 8.

14

Paintings in Lhun Grub Khang

Location

After the gap of about one week alongwith Lama Namgyal I once again visited Matho monastery. It was Friday evening. I went to Lama hostel, Central Institute of Buddhist Studies, Choglamsar. Lama Namgyal was not in his room. However, soon reached. I met and told him about my study plan from which he agreed. After taking permission from Hostel warden he accompanied upto Choglamsar bridge. About 5 O'clock we got Matho minibus and arrived Matho by 5.40 P.M. Thereafter climbing through nearby rocky mountain came in his room. I was completely tired. Namgyal went to his Lama friends and informed them about my planning to study Lhun grub khang in the monastery. We had dinner together and went to bed late right. Next day morning Lama Namgyal brought key from the *comner* of Lhun grub Khang. We started research work on this Dukhang by 9 O'clock.

Lhun grub khang is located at the corner of first floor of the monastery. We climbed through steps near the old Dukhang and came to Verandah. Then went to the Lhakhang. It is also known museum of the monastery.

Paintings

Lhun grub khang has many old ritual things and paintings are made from stone colours. It was built during 16th-17th century. Details of paintings are furnished hereinafter (Fig. 14.1).

1. Kunsel Khorlo[1]

A kind of calender which may be called kun-zang-khorlo.

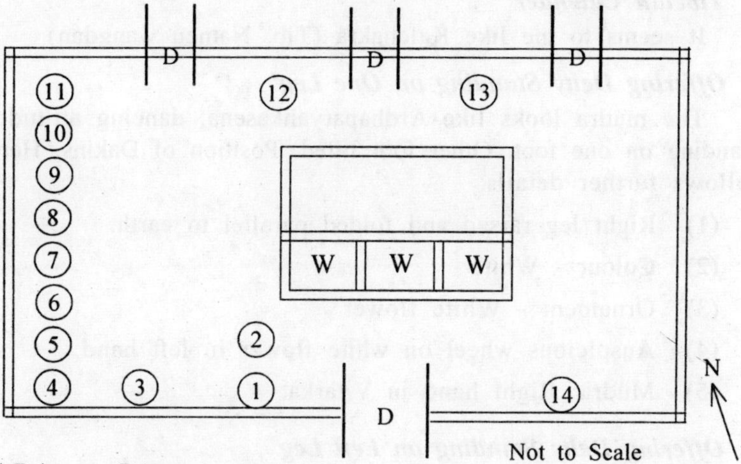

| D | : Door

| | : Wall

W : Window

1 to 14 : Paintings

Fig. 14.1: Wall Paintings in Lhun grub khang.

2. Tokpo Stakthit[2]

It consists of three main items (i) Plant (ii) Sokpo and (iii) Tiger. Here follows further details:

(1) Jewel (Norbu)

(i) *Plant:* Blackish dark green

(ii) *Sokpo:* A Mangolian soldier, who wears the following garments.

- (a) Hat: Red
- (b) Shoes: Red
- (c) Robe: Blue
- (d) Trousers: White
- (e) Symbol: He holds chang pot[3]

(iii) *Tiger:* Golden skin.

3. Tibetan Calender

It seems to me like Kalchakra (Tib. Namcu wangdan)

4. Offering Deity Standing on One Leg[4]

The mudra looks like Ardhaparyankasena, dancing attitude; standing on one foot. Other foot lifted. Position of Dakins. Here follows further details:

(1) Right leg raised and folded parallel to earth.

(2) Colour - White

(3) Ornament - White flower

(4) Auspicious wheel on white flower in left hand.

(5) Mudra: Right hand in Vitarka.

5. Offering Deity Standing on Left Leg

(1) Right leg raised and folded parallel to earth.

(2) *Colour:* Orange

(3) *Mudra:* Left hand holds pungpa on lotus flower, rests near-heart in Vitarka mudra. Right hand raised up near head in Vitarka mudra.

(4) *Crown:* Flowers

(5) *Ornaments:* Anklets, wristlets, necklaces, earring etc. are like Bodhisattva. Besides the flower garland is such a long, touches the lower limbs.

Garments: Blue scarf for upper body. Light blue robe for lower limbs.

(6) *Disc:* standing on moon disc with Padma.

6. Offering Deity Standing on Left Leg

(1) *Colour:* Red

(2) *Mudra:* Both hands rest near heart, palms facing towards front side. Holds flower in left hand.

7. Offering Deity Standing on One Leg in Ardhaparyankasana

(1) *Mudra and Symbol:* Right hand raised up in vitarka mudra. Left hand holds two fishes on padma flower.

(2) *Colour:* Right hand depicted in golden colour and left hand is sky blue.

8. *Offering Deity Standing on One Leg*

(1) *Colour:* Golden

(2) *Mudra:* Dharmacakra. Both hands rest near heart. Left hand holds *Palpue* on white Padma.

9. *Offering Deity Standing on One Leg*

Colour: White

Mudra: Right hand hanging down, palm facing down. Left hand holds *sankha* with flower and middle finger touches thumb tip.

10. *Offering Deity Standing on One Leg*

Colour: Blue

Without flower

Mudra & Symbol: Right hand holds *sankha*. Left hand does not holds any flower, touches third finger tip of thumb.

11. *Offering Deity Standing on One Leg*

Without flower

Colour: Blue

Mudra & Symbol: Holds *Sankha* in right hand. Left hand two fingers fold inside, other facing to earth, and may be called karana mudra.

All the above deities are standing on moon disc on Padma flower with flower garlands and dancing asana.

In the middle Dodyon nga,[5] charya of five senses are depicted by the following symbols.

(1) mirror

(2) Violen

(3) *Sankha* with water

(4) Zalzee

(5) Auspicious cloth

The above Dodyon nga can further expressed as:

(1) Mirror: White with yellow vajra

(2) Violen: Brown colour

(3) White *Sankha*

(4) White zalzee in orange pot

(5) Red cloth.

Upper Side: The following offerings as depicted on the wall are used for tsela namsum[6] prayer.

(1) Yellow pot and yellow *chodpe* with four white things.

(2) Yellow pot full of oranges and four white things

(3) *Sankha* with red scarf

(4) Yellow fruit with green plant

(5) Three standing white flutes tied with red scarf.

(6) *Lungze* inside white

(7) Orange *thodpe* with four white things in yellow pot.

(8) White mirror with orange scarf.

Paintings Just Beneath the Offering Deities

Khadga, blue colour with flames standing on moon disc Padma flower. On left and right sides of Khadga two birds with two heads. The symbol of Lotsava Rinchen zang po, who knows two important languages i.e. Sanskrit and Tibetan very well.

On the Wall Below the Offering Deities

Rinchen nga dun[7] or seven kinds of auspicious things are depicted. They are from left to right listed below.

(1) Yellow cakra on moon disc with flower.

(2) Auspicious jewel with flames standing on white, green, blue and red Padma.

(3) Bstsun rinpoche (Auspicious queen):

Mudra: Right hand in Vitarka. Left hand in cho-chin mudra.

Garments: Red shawl for upper part of the body. Orange samtap for lower limbs.

Asana: Seated on moon disc with white padma. Lalitasana.

(4) Lanpo Rinpoche:

Garments: Hat: White

Upper part of the body: Red shawl

Lower part of the body: Blue robe

Scarf (belt): Green with blue

Mudra and Symbol: Holds jewels in both hands in Dhyana mudra.

Asana: Seated on moon disc, white padma flower.

(5) Lungpo Rinpoche:

Colour: Grey

Vahana: Elephant

Symbol: A jewel on red shawl.

(6) Stak chok Rinpoche:

Colour: Bluish white

Symbol: Jewel on blue-black shade

(7) *Magpon Rinpoche:* Auspicious General

Garments: Warrior's costume

Colour: White

Symbol: Holds sword, depicted as if he is pulling out sword from its cover.

Asana: Seated on white Padma flower.

Face: Fierce with brown.

Paintings on the Centre Wall between Two Doors at North

12. Depicted Various Symbols of Ritual Objects

13. Amitayus[8]

Position: Centre fresco

Mudra: Dhyanasana with pot

Right to the Centre Fresco

(1) A yogi in Dhyana mudra

Left to the Centre Fresco

(2) *Flower plant:* Asoka; red flower with small jagged leaves; symbol of Marichi (yellow), Kurukalla.

(3) *Photang:* A big building for highly respected Lama or for deity.

(4) *Dolma:* She is believed to protect her devotees from many dangers which beset mankind and is widely worshipped.

(5) *Sun and moon:* Sun is in the right side of the centre fresco; symbol of Akasagarbha. Moon, on the left side of the centre fresco, symbol of Sarvani varanaviskambhin.

(6) Buddha, many kinds of animals, Thumpe ponjee and Tsering tukor.

14. Khang Rinpoche

Surrounded by monasteries of various forms.

(1) *Mansarovar lake:* Surrounded by monasteries

(2) *Co:* Three cos are depicted viz. (i) Gonjong co.

(3) Purang Co.

(4) Lhasa Co in a palace.

Frescos in Namling

Facing to the Main Door

(1) Jungpo duljet.[9]

(2) Three lamas.

North Side

(3) Sakyamuni Buddha with his two spiritual disciples Sari and Modgalayayan.

Right Side

(4) Virupa.[10]

(5) Four hands Manjusri.[11]

(6) Left and right sides of Manjusri head lamas of Sakya sect are depicted.

(7) Right corner: White Tara in standing posture.[12]

(8) Left corner: Green Tara in sitting posture.[13]

Towards the Main Door

(9) Sakya Pandita[14]

(10) Guru Rinpoche[15]

11. Sakya head lama

12. Dharmapala in wrathful form.

In brief Lhun grub khang has seventeen century wall paintings. They were made by Kathok Rigzin and Tsewang Norboo of Nyingmapa order.

NOTES AND REFERENCES

1. Kunsel Khorlo: A kind of calender.
2. Tokpo Stakthit: Rigsum gonpo manifestation i.e. of Avalokitesvara, Vajrapani and Manjusri.
3. Chang Pot: In Ladakh, it looks like chang (wine) pot; Vessel or pot.
4. Offering deity standing on one leg. It may be related with Hevajra Tantra.
5. Dodyon nga: Tib. 'adod-yon-sna-lnga.

   They are five indriyas i.e. five sensitive organs. In Tibetan spell as (i) gzugs (ii) sgra (iii) dri (iv) ro and (v) rig-bya.
6. tsela namsum (or tshe lha rnam gsum): They are (i) tshe dpag med (ii) rnam rgyal ma and (iii) grol ma.

7. Rinchen nga dun: Tib. rin chen ceda bdun. Pron. rinchen seda dun. The name of these jewels are:
   (a) Wheel (*cakra*), Tib. 'khor lo
   (b) Jewel (*ratna*), Tib. nor bu
   (c) Queen (*rani*), Tib. cun mo
   (d) Civil Minister (*Mantri*), Tib. blon po
   (e) Elephant, usually white (*hathi*), Tib. glang po che
   (f) Horse (*asva*); rta mchog.
   (g) Military commander (*Senapati*); Tib. dmag dpon.

   The above seven jewels are associated with world ruler and also with a Buddha.
8. Amitayus: He is the`lord Buddha of longevity or the Bodhisattva of longevity who is invoked for long life, health and happiness. He has one face, two arms in dhyana mudra, holding an vase with the elixir of life; a golden vase containing the nectar of immortality and a spring of the myrohalan plant. Cf. Bunce, Fredrick W. : *An Encyclopaedia of Buddhist Deities,* 1994: 13.
9. Jungpo duljet: A kind of Mahakala; the great black one" The universal protector."
10. Virupa: He is equivalant Virupa, a Mahasiddha has one face, calm, wide eyes, floral wealth; arms, two, right hand holds surya, left hand holds kapala.
11. Four hands Manjusri: Tib. 'Jam dbyangs. He is the Bodhisattva of wisdom and is considered by the Northern Buddhists as one of the eight Dhyani Bodhisattvas. With his sword he destroys ignorance and darkness. He was one of the eight chief disciples of Sakyamuni who used to raise questions concerning the emptiness for the benefit of other listeners.
12. White Tara: She is a female tutelary deity in compassion's motherly form. She embodies the fertile aspects of compassion and her realm is the day. In her "Ordinary" white form she is represented by Astamahabhaya--Tara and Mrityuvancana Tara. She sits in the full lotus posture on moon and sun discs upon lotus flower. Cf. Bruce, Fredrick W.: *'An Encyclopaedia of Buddhist Deities, Demigods, Godlings, Saints and Demons,'* Vol. I, DK Printworld Ltd., New Delhi. 1994: 524 - '43.
13. Green Tara: Tib. grol ma ljang gu Pron Drolma Jang-gu or "green savioress" is probably the form of Tara incarnate in Wencheng, the Chinese wife of king Songtsen Gompo. She is green, sits in

the royal posture on the moon disc and lotus flower. Cf. Finegan, Jack: *Tibet: A Dreamt of Image,* Tibet House, New Delhi, 1986: 136.

14. Sakya Pandita: In Tibetan equivalent Kun-dga' rgyal mtshan (kunga Gyenten). He was born in 1182 A.D. Later became abbot of Sakya order and after attaining reputation in Buddhist philosophy called Sakya Pandita "the learned Sakya scholar," Cf. Finegan, Jack, *op. cit.*: 105.

15. Guru Rinpoche: Popularly known as Padmasambhava. He was the great mystic saint from India who had tremendous miraculous powers. He brought Buddhist Tantra in Tibet during 8th century A.D. and introduced its learning and practice. He is venerated by the Tibetans as the Second Buddha. Cf. Lobzang Tsewang: *'Sakyamuni,'* CIBS, 2001: 26.

15

Thankas in Lhun Grub Khang

It is remarkable to note that as a unique type of painting called scroll painting or Thanka (or Thang-ka) is a painting on cloth. It portrays various forms of divinities or groups of divinities. These are carried by monks in religious procession and used to decorate homes. They represent the deities surrounded by groups of lesser deities and scenes from the lives of Tibetan saints and teachers. In Ladakh it is a custom to make thankas in order to recover from sickness when somebody dies. The popular thankas thus based on Buddha and Bodhisattvas viz. Avalokitesvara, Dolma, Manjusri, Vajrapani etc.

In Lhun grub khang the following thankas are hanged through ceiling of Namling.

1. *Yamantaka Thanka:* Yamantaka is one of the Dharmapalas; chos-skyon (Tib. Chho-chyong); Defender of the faith. It is also named as g'Sing-rje g'sed (Shin-ji she). Conqueror of death, Vajrabhairava. Form is the manifestation of Manjusri. He is the 'Destroyer of death' belongs to the supreme yoga tantra division of Vajrayana and is the protector of Geluk pa order. Face: Nine, the central face is bull's face with two horns and its complexion is dark and in the angry form. This form symbolizes the ignorance which is transmitted into discriminating wisdom. The second face is of demon and the top face is Manjusri which is in peaceful form. Each face has three eyes and wrathful form. Through his faces, he can look in all directions. Hands: Thirty four, two principal embrace Shakti, hold skull-cup and ritual chopper. Body yab-

yum. Legs: sixteen. Stepping on human bodies or evil spirits. Shakti – complexion is dark, has two hands, one face and three eyes. Ornaments: Five skull crown, wristlets, anklets, necklace, garlands, and belt 8 skulls tiger skin as body covering.[1]

2. The thanka of head lama of Sakya order. He is surrounded by the mandala of Sakya lamas and associated deities. It is hanged at the Right of the Yamantaka Thanka.

3. Avalokitesvara four-arms Thanka is at the left of the Yamantaka Thanka. In this Thanka Avalokitesvara is the central figure, surrounded by Bodhisattvas in his mandala. The main figure has one head and four arms. Seated in dhyanasana on lotus throne; high Usnisa with a flaming pearl; two original hands in namaskar mudra; his other hands hold mala and Padma. Sometimes pustaka at shoulder levels.

Lhun grub khang has only a few thankas, which are small in size about 3' x 2' each. They are in a very bad condition and needed to proper preservation, some cracks and turns are also noted. For possible repair by expert local artists, only local original colours should be used.

NOTES AND REFERENCES

1. Natchelor, Stephen: *The Tibet Guide,* Wisdom Pub., London, 1987: 409-'10; Lobzang Tsewang:' *Sakyamuni: An Exhibition of Rare Thankas'*, CIBS, Leh-Ladakh, 2001 : 34 and Bunce, Fredric W. *'An Encyclopaedia of Buddhist Deities, Demigods, Godlings, Saints and Demons'*, Vol. I, D.K. Printworld Ltd., New Delhi, 1994 : 574.

16

Statues in Lhun Grub Khang

In this temple Buddhist statues are along the North-west side wall and are preserved in the glass almirah (Fig. 16.1)

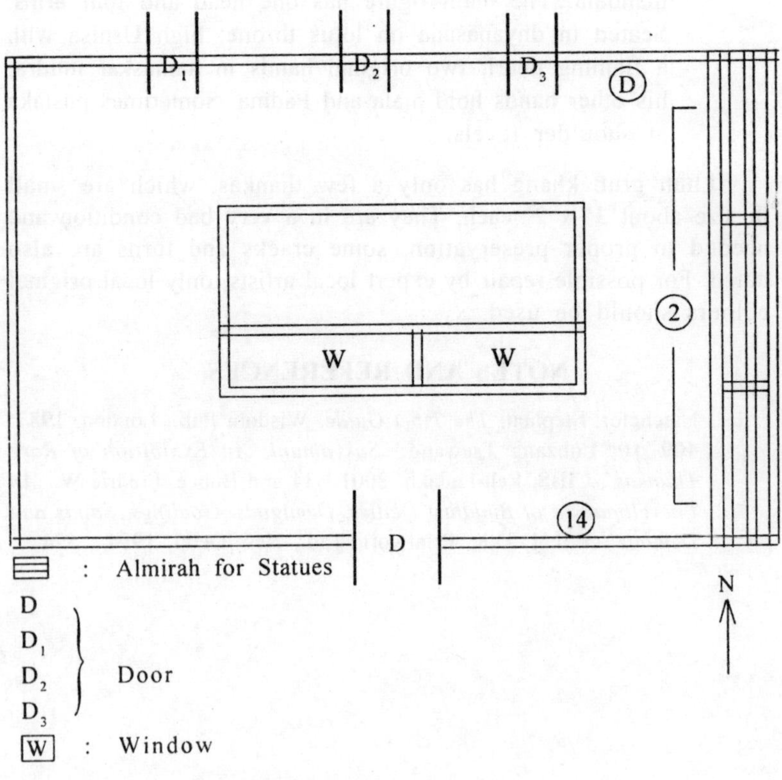

Fig. 16.1: Statues in Lhun Grub Khang

Here follows the details:

North Side Wall in Front of the Main Door

(1) ***Maitreya:*** Seated

Height – 5 feet

Colour – Yollowish

(2) ***West side wall:***

Main Statue: Norchen Dorje chang kunga zangpo:[2] He is the founder of Ngorpa sect of Sakya.

Mudra: Dharmacakra

Hat: Red

Face: Golden

Body: Golden

Chosgos: Orange

Asana: Seated, probably Dhyanasana

Height: 4' 3"

Width: 3'

Statues in the Almirah

(a) Right Side of the Main Statue in Upper Shelf: Head lama of Sakya

Mudra: Right hand in Dharmacakra mudra, Left hand in Meditation.

Hat: Red

Chosgos: Orange

Asana: Seated on throne, may be in Dhyanamudra

Height: 27" (with throne from the base)

Width: 1' 5" (with throne)

(b) Left to Head Lama of Sakya Order

(1) Dogon Chosgyal Phagspa:[3] A Sakya Lama

Hat: Red

Chosgos: Red

Body: Yellow

Asana: Seated on Padma throne

Mudra: Touches first finger with thumb and rest both arms near heart, Dharmachakra.

Height: 10" (with throne)

(2) Next to Dogon Chosgyal Phagspa: Padmasambhava[4]

Height: 4"

(3) Unidentified Statue

This is a small statue placed in front of the throne.

Below the Above Statues in Almirah

(4) Padmasambhava:

Height – 3' 4"

Asana – Seated in Dhyanasana

Width – 2' 8" (with throne)

(c) Right Behind Padmasambhava:

Maitreya:

Asana: About to stand

Height: 2' 6" (with throne)

(1) 'Hum" Carved Stone

One letter 'Hum' of 'Om Mani Padme Hum'[5] is carved on a preice of stone. It is placed in front of the above statue.

(d) Upper Shelf of the Almirah

(i) Buddha with Sari and Modgalyayan[6]

Budda: He is seated with lungzet (pot) at the centre of his lap.

Mudra: Dhyana: Right hand in Bhumisparsha. Left hand holds lungzet in Dhyana.

Both spiritual disciples Sariputra and Modgalayayan are standing at right and left of Buddha.

(e) In Front of Buddha

(i) Dogon chosgyal Phagspa:

Height – 5"

(f) Below Sakya Head Lama in the Almirah: Maitreya

Asana: About to stand

Height: 3' 4" with throne of Padma Mudra.

(g) Upper Side in Almirah

Small Statues:

(1) Vajrapani[7]

(2) Avalokitesvara[8]

(3) Manjusri[9]: Two in number

(4) Dolma[10]

(5) Dolma

(6) Avalokitesvara: Height – 6"

(7) Not identified: Height – 5"

(8) Not identified: —

} These statues are placed from left to right.

(h) Below the Above Statues

(1) Amitayus:[11]

Asana: Seated, Dhyanasana.

Mudra: Meditation, with pot of longevity

Height: 4' 3" with the base of throne

Width: 2' 10"

(i) Behind the Amityus

Right side: Avalokitesvara:

Asana: Meditation

Height: 4' 3"

Hands: Two right hand holds rosary.

Right in Upper Side

1. Avalokitesvara:

Hands: Four

Asana: Meditation

Height: 2' 5"

2. Head Lama of Sakya Order:

Position: Ahead of Avalokitesvara

Height: 2'

Hat: Red

Chosgos: Red

Body colour: Golden

Other cloths: Red

3. A Sakya lama
4. Dolma
5. Buddha
6. Amitayus

} These are small statues about each 6" in height

(j) In the Lower Shelf of Almirah

Statue: Maritreya

Asana: About to stand

Height: 3' 4"

Right to Maitreya

Changchub Chorten[12]

Height: 3' 4"

(k) Left to the Main Statue

Left to Right

(1) Virupa[13]

Hat: Red

Symbols: Holds yellow flower in one hand and golden flower in other.

Asana: Seated

Height: 4"

(2) Head Lama of the Sakya Tradition

Hat: Red

Garments: Upper part of the body is covered by red shawl and lower part by red robe.

Asana: Seated

Height: 2' 7" with throne

Width: 2'

Below Head Lama of Sakya Tradition

(3) Lama of Sakya

Hat: Red

Garments: Red

Stotgag: Red

Body: Yellow

Posture: Seated

Height: 3' with throne

Width: 2" 7"

(l) Upper Side to the Head Lama of Sakya

1. Changchub chorten
2. Buddha (Co-Rinpoche)

   Mudra: Left hand holds *patra* in Dhyana mudra. Right hand in Bhumisparsha.

   Height: 2' 7"

   Width: 2'

   Ahead to Buddha: From Right to Left

1. Manjusri
2. Manjusri
3. Six handed Mahakala[14]

4. Medicine Buddha[15]
5. Height: 4" to 5"

(m) Below Chepakmet

Buddha

Asana: Meditation

Height: 2' 10"

Width: 2' 3"

There is a footprint of high ranked lama on a stone, placed behind the chepakmed.

(n) Upper Shelf of the Almirah

1. Avalokitesvara
2. Avalokitesvara
3. Avalokitesvara
4. Avalokitesvara

These are placed from left to right of Padmasambhava and all are in 4" in height

Below Shelf

Statue: Manjusri seated in dhyanasana Mudra : Dharmachakra, holds Padma stem with flowers of at shoulder level supporting Khadga and Pustaka.

Crown: Five

Hands: Two

Height: 4' 4"

Width: 3'

(o) Upper Shelf

Unidentified Statue Looks as Birupa

Body: Blue

Posture: Seated

(p) Right to the Above Statue

Five Vajra kilas supported with wooden stand

Vajrapani:[16] Two in number, wrathful

Height: 2' 10"
Width: 1'

Besides these some small Buddhist statues are placed before the window of Namling of the same temple. They are listed below:

1. Thirty five Buddhas, teaching mudra, 6" in height and seated on Padma throne.
2. Three Avalokitesvara, each has four hands and seated on Padma throne.
3. Namgyal Chorten.

NOTES AND REFERENCES

1. Maitreya: He is regarded as a future Buddha who will come down to the world to liberate the sentient being when Sakyamuni's teachings will disappear from the earth. is believed that at present, he lives in the Tusita Loka in the form of a Bodhisattva. Cf. Lobzang Tseuwang; 'Sakyamuni: *An Exhibition of Rare Thankas,'* Central Institute of Buddhist Studies, Leh-Ladakh, 200-24.
2. Norchen Dorje chang kunga zangpo, Sakya Lama of Mahayana Buddhism.
3. Dogon chosgyal Phagspa: Sakya Lama of Mahayana Buddhism.
4. Padmasambhava: Tib. Lopon Rinpoche or Gur Rinpoche. "Lotus Born One," an Indian Tantric invited by king Trisong detsen in the Eighth Century A.D. He propagated Buddhist Tantra in Tibet during the above period and subdued the local deities and demons while constructing the Samyas monastery in Tibet. Cf. Batchelor Stepheni: *The Tibet Guide,* Wisdom Pub., London; 1987 : 420.
5. Om Mani Padme Hum: It is a Avalokitesvara mantra.
6. Buddha with Sari and Modgalayayan: Tib. Shakya Tubpa Pron. Tubgpa. Historically known as Gotama Buddha. After attaining enlightenment at Bodhgaya, he turned the three wheel of Dharma in three places viz. Varanasi, Gridrakuta and Vaisali. Besides, he went to Tusita loka and preached god, goddess and his mother. It is said that he turned the wheel of tantra at Dhanyakuta by manifesting himself into Vijradhara.

7. Vajrapani: Tib. Phyag-na-rdo-rje- tho-drug-pa, Pron. Eng. Phyag-dor, one of a triad of mountain deities known as rigs gsum mgon-po-and includes: spyan-ras gziggy and 'gam-dpal dbyangs. He is the Bodhisativa of energy and power. Cf. Bunce, Fredric W.: *An Encyclopaedia of Buddhist Demigods;* Vol. I, D.K. Print World, 1994: 397.
8. Avalokitesvara: The Buddha of compassion, is the chief Bodhisattva of Mahayana Buddhism. Literally: A Mahabodhisattva and one of the most popular Bodhisattvas in the world of Budhism. Cf. Bunce, Frederick W.: *An Encyclopaedia of Buddhist Deities, op. cit.*, 1994: 36.
9. Manjusri: Arya Manjusri. He is the embodiment of the wisdom of all the Buddhas. According to one tradition, he attained perfect enlightenment countless aeon back. Cf. Lobzang Tsenwang: *'Sakyamuni,'* CIBS, Leh Ladakh, 2001: 22.
10. Dolma: In Sanskrit equivalent to Tara. She is the female Bodhisattva and is regarded as the manifestation of Avalokitesvara. She is worshipped as the bestower of life and protector, for those who are frightened with the eight elements of fear.
11. Amitayus. Tib. Ts'e dpag-med, Tshe – dpag-med, che-dpag-med, Tshe-dpag – med – lha – dgu, (Pron Eng. Tsepame." Dispenser of long life.") The Bodhisattva of longevity who is invoked for long life, health and happiness. Cf. Bunce, Fredrick W.: *An Encyclopaedia of Buddhist Deities,* Vol. I, D.K. Printworld Ltd., New Delhi, 1994: 13.
12. Chang chub Chorten: In Hindi language chorten is equivalent 'Stupa' which literally means an "offering holder." The 'Changchub' means chorten of illumination.
13. Virupa: He is equivalent Virupa, a Mahasiddha from whom Havajra tantras transmitted to Sakya lama of Mahayana.
14. Six hands Mahakala: Tib. Mgon po phyag drug pa, Myur-mdzad-ye-shes-kyi-mgon po-phyag – drugpa. One of the Dharmapala. He has one face, three eyes, fierce, flame like hair and six arms. Cf. Bunce, Fredrick W.: *'An Encyclopaedia of Buddhist Deities, Demigods, Godlings, Saints and Demons,' op. cit.*, 1994: 464.
15. Medicine Buddha: Tib. Sangye Menlha, in Sanskrit equivalent to Baisajytaguru. The Medicine Buddha is the Buddha of healing, who is invoked to care for the sick. He wears the monastic robes of a Buddha and sits on a lotus blossom upon a lion throne. His

body is dark blue and he holds an iron bowl in his left hand containing the medicinal plant arura. He may also hold a stem of the arura plant in his right hand. Cf. Bune, Fredric W.: *'An Encyclopaedia of Buddhist Deities, Demigods, Godlings, Saints and Demon,' op. cit.*, 1994: 338.

16. Vajrapani. supra. No. 7.

17

Lhun Grub Khang: A Museum

In Lhum grub khang, many antiques are preserved in glass almirah. There are some masks along the window of Namling. Details are furnished in the following table.

TABLE 17.1

Antiques in Lhun Grub Khang

Sl. No.	*Name of item*	*Identification*	*Number*
1.	Kale Kave	Mask	01
2.	Gonpo[1]	Mask	01
3.	Phumet	Charm dress	01
4.	Turthot[2]	Charm Cap	02
5.	Yamantaka[3]	Mask	01
6.	Che-chang	Mask (member of Gonpo mandala)	01
7.	Skyespa		02
8.	Black Cup	Mask	02
9.	Deities Weapons	—	—
10.	Pots[4]	Symbol	—
11.	Bell Covers[5]	Symbol	—
12.	Tung (Sankha)[6]	Symbol	—
13.	Vajra Kalika[7]	Symbol	—
14.	Sword cover[8]	Symbol	—
15.	Tranbed	—	—
16.	Masks	Symbol	02
17.	Printing blocks[9] (Kangyur & Stangur Religious pothis were printed from them)	Wooden blocks	02
18.	Shoes of Oracles[10]	—	02

19.	Tiger skin used[11] during Nangrang by Lhas	—	01
20.	Hat of oracles[12]	—	02
21.	Pungpa Cover	—	—
22.	Tung Cover	—	—
15.	Janak mask hat[13]	—	01
16.	Effigy of Yak[14]	—	01

Source: On the spot study by the author during 2006- 07.

NOTES AND REFERENCES

1. Gonpo: He is the Dharmapala. There are many forms of Gonpo viz. Two hands Gonpo, Four hands gonpo, Six handed gonpo etc. In Sanskrit he is equivalent to Mahakala.
2. Turthot: Turdok cap, but it is relate with dress only.
3. Yamantaka: He is also called as yamadaka. In Sanskrit equivalent to Vajrabhairava. He is the most wrathful form of Manjusri, and is considered the embodiment of total wrath.
4. Pot (Patra): Begging bowl; symbol of Amitabha, Man-la, Gautama, and Avalokitesvara. Cf. Gordan, K Antoinette: *"The Iconography of Tibetan Lamaism,'* Munshiram Manoharlal Pub. Ltd., New Delhi, 1998: 16.
5. Bell Cover: In fact Bell is the symbol of ritual object. Bell with vajra handle; symbol of Vajradhara, Vajrasattva, Trailokyavijaya and yidam. Cf. Gordan, K. Antoinatte; *op.cit.* 14.
6. Sankha (Tib. Tung): Conch shell, used as a trumpet; symbol of Vajratara and Ekajata. Cf. Gorden, K. Antoinette; *op. cit.*: 18.
7. Vajra Kalika (or Vajra), thunderbolt (literally, diamond) scepter; symbol of Akodbhya, Vajrapani, Vajradhara, Vajrasattva and all yi-dam. Cf. Gordan, K. Antoinette, *op. cit.*, 18.
8. Sword cover: The sword or khadga is the symbol of Manjusri, Karmadakini, Chuda, Avalokitesvara (Tantric), Mahasahasda—pramardani and Mahamayuri. Cf. Gorden, K. Antoinette, *op.cit.*, 14.
9. Printing blocks: These wooden Printing blocks are used for printing Buddhist texts and for religious flags.
10. Shoes of Oracles: During Nangrang, the scared dance Rongtsan deities wear these shoes.

11. Tiger skin used during by lhas:
12. Hat of Oracles: During Rongtsan deities wear the hat.
13. Janak mask hat: During cham Janak mask is wore by lama and perform cham during the festival.
14. Effigy of Yak: Yak is a famous animal of Ladakh. It is used for carrying load from one place to other through high passes.

18

Statues in Kangyur Lhakhang

This Lhakhang has two poles, two windows, Kangyur pothis, one changchub chorten and some Buddhist statues. An elaborate description is presented in the following Fig. 18.1.

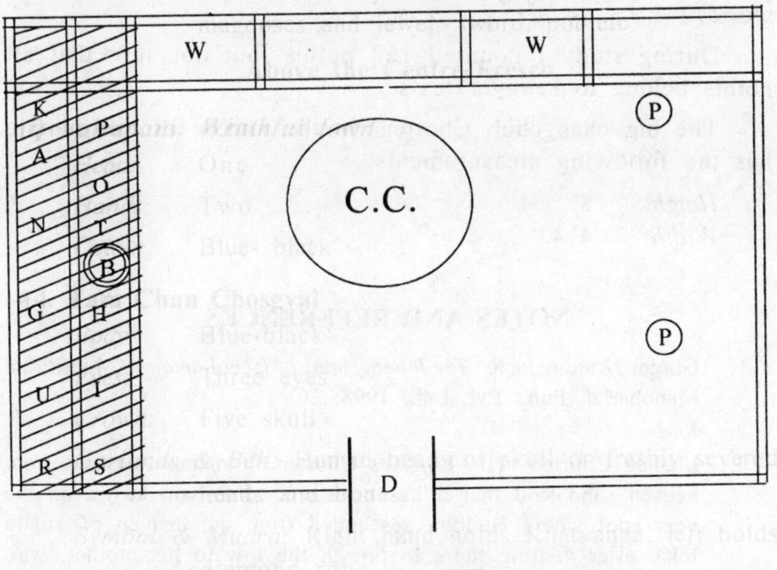

(C.C.) : Chanchup Chorten

(P) : Pole

| D | : Door

| | : Wall

W : Window

(hatched) : Kangyur Pothis

(B) : Centre Statue

Fig. 18.1: Statues in Kangyur Lhakhang.

Kangyur Lhakhang has only one Buddha statue, which has following measurements:

Height: 3' 3" (with throne)

Width: 2' 8"

Mudra: One hand is in Bhumisparsa, and other Dhyana mudra. Bhumisparsa can be witnessed as: Earth touching. Right arm is pendant over right knee. Hand, palm inward, all fingers down, is touching lotus throne.[1]

The other hand is in Dhyana mudra, which means all fingers of the concern extended and palms up.[2]

Besides, it has one Lhabab chorten,[3] which is built by sandal wood.

During study I counted 162 pothis, but not sure that all pothis belong to kangyur texts.[4]

The big changchub Chorten[5] in the middle of this temple has the following measurements:

Height: 8'

Width: 4' 4."

NOTES AND REFERENCES

1. Gordon, Antoinette K.: *The Iconography of Tibet Lamaism,* Munshiram Manoharlal, Pub., Pvt. Ltd., 1998: 20.
2. *Ibid.*
3. Lhabab Chorten: Tib. Lhababs Chorten. It means "descent from heaven" and said that it has been erected at sam kasya, on the very spot where Buddha descended from the heaven of Tusita loka, after visiting there to preach the low to his mother, who had ascended there after her death. In this Chorten all four sides, or sometimes only one side there are steps.
4. Kangyur texts. King Trhisong Desen during 8th century A.D. did a very important work for the collection of various Buddhist texts. These were later edited by Buston and the entire body of texts divided into two parts. The first part is the bka 'gyur (Pron. Kangyur), which means" translation of the Buddha speech". Cf.

Finegan, Jack: *Tibet: A Dreamt of Image,* Tibet House, New Delhi, 1986, pp. 14-15.

5. Changchub Chorten: Tib. Byan-cub – mcod rten. It means chorten of illumination. It has square base with one more steps round the foot; above this is a round drum, the bum pa or 'pot'; above this again are seven or thirteen 'umbrella,' mounted on a central axis which traverses of them; and at the top of the whole structure is a metal ring, usually gilded, supporting a crescent and circle which respectively represent the moon and the sum.

19

Thankas in Kangyur Lhakhang

There are few thankas in this Lhakhang. They are hanged through the ceiling and along the poles. Here follows the details: *On the eight side wall along the door.*

1. Rahula Tib. Tho Bzhi Pa[1]

Height: 5' 8" with border silk cloth

Width: 4' with border silk cloth

Thanka without border cloth

Height: 3' 8"

Width: 2' 11"

2. Buddha Amitabha[2]

Body Colour: Red

Mudra: Meditation with *lungze*

Thanka with border cloth

Height: 5' 11"

Width: 3' 7"

Thanka without border cloth

Height: 3' 9"

Width: 2' 10"

In the mandala various deities/Bodhisattvas are depicted.

3. Unidentified Thanka with Border Cloth

Height: 5'

Width: 3'

Thanka without border cloth

Height: 3' 7"

Width: 2' 6"

4. *Buddha, thanka with border cloth*

Height: 4' 4"

Width: 3'

Mudra: Bhumisparsha and Dhyana mudra.

Manda: Surrounded by Buddhas with different mudras

Thanka without border cloth

Height: 3'

Width 1' 6"

5. *Vajradhara,[3] thanka with border cloth*

Height: 4' 7"

Width: 3'

Mudra & Symbols: Vajrahumkara, Buddha supreme and Eternal; wrist crossed at breast, holding Vajra and Ghanta.

Mandala: At the top

Sakya Pandita,[4] Other Sakya lamas.

Thanka without border cloth

Height : 3' 4"

Width: 2' 7"

Below the above thanka, the following paintings on the wall are depicted.

From Right to Left

(i) Kurukulla: Tib. Ku-ru-ku-le or ku-ru-ku-li thal mo brgyal pa. The red Tara and a popular goddess. In Ladakh she is popularly known goddess of riches.

Face: One, angry, three eyes

Hands: Four
Principal hands draw leafed bow and arrow
Right hand holds hook
Left hand holds lotus

Body: Mature, nude

Legs: Two

Asana: Ardhadparyankasana and stepped on human corpse/demon.

Height: 3'

Width: 4' 8"

(ii) *Chogdak*[6]

Hands: 12

Asana: Standing on left leg and right leg hand parallel to the earth; Ardhaparyani Aasana.

(iii) *Dhodgyal*[7]

Mudra: Yab-yum; tantric deity.

All the above frescos are standing on sun disc.

Some thankas are hanged with the poles. The details are as follows:

6. *Vajrasattva*[8]

In the mandala on the top karpo Namsum lama is depicted.

Thanka with border cloth

Height: 4' 2"

Width: 2' 10"

Thanka without border cloth

Height: 3' 3"

Width: 2' 6"

7. *Rigsum Gonpo*[9]

Mudra: Peaceful

Asana: Standing

Thanka with border cloth

Height: 3' 9"

Width: 2' 9"

Thanka without border

Height: 2' 5"

Width: 2' 2"

Along Window Right to Left

8. Buddha Amitabha

Colour: Red with Rainbow hallow around the head.

Asana: Dhyana

Height: 5' 5" with silk cloth border

Width: 3' 2"

Without Border Cloth

Height: 3' 3"

Width: 2' 9"

9. Lama Tagsang[10]

Dress/ornament: Two *Kundal*

Mudra: Dhyanasana, Right hand in Bhumisparsha. Left hand in Dhyana with jewel.

Mandala: The following Buddha and Bodhisattvas are depicted.

(i) *Buddha:* On the top left corner
(ii) *Buddha:* On the top right corner
(iii) *Vajrapani:* Below at the right corner
(iv) *Gonkar:* Below at the left corner, holds sword.

With Silk Cloth Border

Height: 4' 2"

Width: 2' 10"

Without Silk Cloth Border

Height: 2' 9"

Width: 2' 3"

***10. Dolkar*[11]**

Colour: White

Painting style: Ties (chis)

With Silk Cloth Border

Height: 4' 5"

Width: 3'

Without Silk Cloth Border

Height: 2' 7"

Width: 2'

11. Opakmed*[12] *(with silk border cloth)

Height: 3' 10"

Width: 2' 10"

Without Silk Border Cloth

Height: 2' 6"

Width: 2' 4"

12. Avalokitesvara*[13] *(with silk border cloth)

Height: 3' 10"

Width: 2' 9"

Hands: Four

Asana: Dhyanasama

Without Silk Cloth Border

Height: 2' 6"

Width: 2' 2"

13. Namtosras*[14] *or God of Wealth

With Silk Border Cloth

Height: 4' 7"

Width: 3'

Without Silk Cloth Border

Height: 3' 5"

Width: 2' 8"

NOTES & REFERENCES

1. Rahula (Tib. Tho bzhi pa): One of the sixteen Arhats of Sakyamuni Buddha who had attained the first stage of Nirvana.
2. Buddha Amitabh: He is the Buddha of Infinite light, is known as the fourth of the Dhyani Buddha Families, the embodiment of compassion. He is widely worshipped by the Buddhists where Mahayana Buddhism existed. Cf. Tara, CIBS, 2002:20. (Leh-Ladakh)
3. Vajradhara: Tib. Dorje Chang. He is the tantric manifestation of Sakyamuni Buddha. He has one face, two arms which carry Vajra and bell in Vajrahumkara mudra. Cf. Bunce, Fredrick W.: *An Encyclopaedia of Buddhist Deities...* Vol, I, D.K. Printworld Ltd., New Delhi, 1994: 577
4. Sakya Pandita: He was the abbot of Sakya order during 13th century A.D., was born in 1182, under his direction Sakya-pa attained political supremacy in Tibet.
5. Kurukulla: Tib. Ku-ru-ku-le or ku-ru-ku-li-thal-mo-brgyal pa. The red Tara and a popular goddess. In Ladakh she is popularly known as goddess of riches.
6. Chogdak: Tib. Tshogs-bdag-dmar can. He has one face, three eyes and one tusk; hands: Twelve; Vahana: Mouse on red lotus. Cf. Bunce, Fredric W: *'An Encyclopadiea of Buddhist Deities...'* Vol. I, D.K. Print World, New Delhi, 1994, pp. 164-'65.
7. Dhodgyal: Sungma (Dharma Protector).
8. Vajrasattva: Tib. Rdo-rje-sems-dpa, rdo-rje-sems-dpah, byan-chub-rch-rje-sems-dpah, (Pron. Eng. Dorje Sempa). The ultimate Bodhisattva of purification and the awareness of Ultimate reality.
9. Rigsum Gonpo: Tib. Sigs gsum mgon po. They are three Bodhisattvas, namely.
   (1) Avalokitesvara (Tib. Spyen ras gzigs)
   (2) Manjusri (Tib. 'ajam p'ai dbyangs)
   (3) Vajrapani (Tib. Phyag rdor): He is the Bodhisattva. In Tibetan language equivalent Phyag na-rdo-rje, Pron. Chhana Dorje. He is a manifestation of Aklshobya, and is usually shown as dark blue in colour.
10. Lama Tagsang: Tag tsang belongs to Drug pa tradition of Mahayana.
11. Dolkar or grol ma dkar po phon. Eng. (grolma karpo). She embodies the fertile aspects of compassion and her realm is the day. She is represented by Astamahabhaya Tara.

12. Opakmed (or 'Od-dpag-med, hod-dpag-med), (Pron. Eng. Opagme). In Sanskrit equivalent to Amitabha "Immeasurable light" or "Infinite light."
13. Avalokitesvara: Tib. Chenrezi or Chenrazi. A Mahabodhisattva and one of the most popular Bodhisattvas in the world of Buddhism.
14. Namtosras or Nam-thos-sras; rgyal po rnam thos sras; (Pron. English Namtose). A guardian King in Sanskrit equivalent to Devaraja; Lokapala of the northern quarter of the world.

20

Statues in Lham Das Khang

In this temple Buddhist statues are placed along the eastern side wall. Here on the north side has two windows and one pole at the centre. Details are furnished hereinafter (Fig. 20.1).

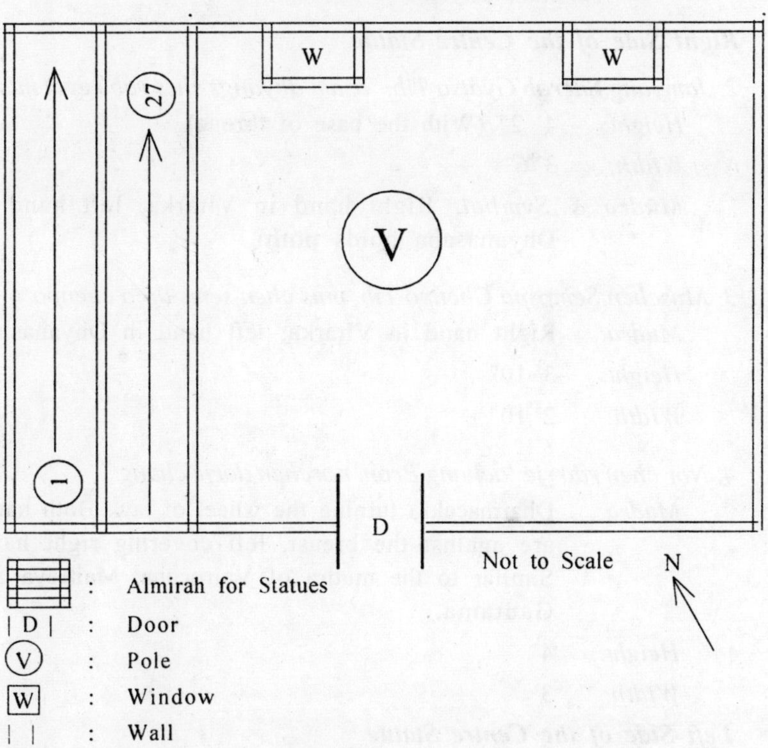

Fig. 20.1: Statues in Lham Das Khang.

Right to Left

Below the Glass Almirah

1. 'agro mgon chos rgyal 'aphags pa (Pron. Dogon chogyal phagspa)

Position: Centre Statue

Material: Clay

Height: 4' 5" (with the base of throne)

Width: 3' 7"

Garments: Lama dress with red hat

Mudra: Right hand in Bhumisparsha, left hand in Dhyana with jewel.

Right Side of the Centre Statue

2. Jamyang Sherab Gyatso Tib. 'azam dbyangs shes rab rgyal mtso

Height: 4' 2" (With the base of throne)

Width: 3' 6"

Mudra & Symbol: Right hand in Vitarka, left hand in Dhyanasana holds pothi.

3. Muschen Sempspa Chenpo Tib. mus chen sems dp'a chenpo

Mudra: Right hand in Vitarka, left hand in Dhyanasana

Height: 3' 10"

Width: 2' 10"

4. Nor chen rdo rje 'achang Pron. norchen dorje chang

Mudra: Dharmacakra turning the wheel of law. Both hands are against the breast, left covering right hand. Similar to the mudra of Vairocana, Maitreya and Gautama.

Height: 4'

Width: 3'

Left Side of the Centre Statue

5. Khasdup Paldan Dorje Tib. mkhas grub dpal ldan rdo rje

Position: Left side first to the centre statue.

Height: 4' 2"

Width: 3' 8"

Mudra: Right hand in Vitarka, left hand in Dhyana mudra.

6. Gorampa Sonam Senge (Tib. Kun mkhyen go ram pa bsod nams senge)

Mudra: Right hand in Vitarka, left hand in Dhyana mudra.

Height: 4'

Width: 2' 10"

*7. Lama chakyi Lotos (*Tib. *Bla ma chos blo gros)*

Mudra: Right hand in Vitarka, left hand in Dhyana mudra

Height: 3' 7"

Width: 2' 9"

8. Namgyal Chorten

Position: Right side

Height: 2'

Width: 7"

9. There are many small Buddha statues ahead to the central statue.

On the Left Side In Front of the Gorampa Sonam

There are some more Buddhist Statues.

10. Sachan Kunga Nying po: They are three in number.

11. Sakya Pandita

12. Dogon Chosgyal phagspa

They are two in number

13. Zambala

14. Unidentified lama

He has beard. All the statues from 10 to 14, are 8" to 10" in height.

15. Upper shelf of the Almirah

16. Buddha:

Position: Central statue

Height: 3'

Width: 2' 10"

Mudra: Right hand in Bhumisparsha mudra, left hand in Dhana mudra.

Right Side of the Central Statue

17. Tungpa Dorje Palzang Tib. Dung dpalzang pa rdo-rje bzang po

Height: 3'

Width: 2'8"

Mudra: Right hand in Bhumisparsha, left hand in Dhyana mudra with pot.

18. Yong zin Konchog Phelwa (Tib. Yongs 'azin dkon mchog 'aphel ba)

Height: 2' 9"

Width: 2' 3"

Mudra: Right hand in Bhumisparsha, left hand in meditation with pot.

19. Dorje chang

Colour: Blue

Symbol and Mudra: Holds dorje in both hands.

Height: 2' 8"

Width: 10"

20. Konchog Lhundup (Tib. Dkon mchog lhungrup)

Height: 2' 9"

Width: 2" 4"

Mudra: Right hand in Bhumisparsha, left hand in Dhyana with pothi.

21. Birupa.

Colour: Brown

Height: 2' 6"

Mudra: Right hand up in Tarjani mudra.

Height: 2' 6"

Width: 11"

22. *Jetsun Sanges Rinchen (Tib. Rje btsun sangs rgyas rin chen)*

Height: 2' 9"

With: 2' 3"

Mudra: Right hand in Vitarka mudra, left hand in Dhana with fruit pot.

Left to the Central Statue

23. *Jetsum Gongma namnga: These are as follows:*

(i) Sachan kunga nying po

(ii) Sonam tsemo

(iii) Jetsun dakpa gyaltsan

(iv) Sakya pandita kung ga gyaltsan

(v) Dogon chos gyal phagspa

All the above five statues are having the following measurements.

Height: 10"

Width: 10"

24. *Gyalwa Lhachog Sange*

Mudra: Right hand in Vitarka mudra, left hand in Dhyana.

Height: 2' 10"

Width: 2' 6"

25. *Norchen Dorje Chang*

Height: 2' 7"

Width: 9"

Mudra: Dharmacakra mudra

26. Dogon Chosgyal phagspa

Height: 2'

Width: 8"

Mudra: Right hand in Vitarka mudra, left hand in Dhyana

27. *Gonpo: In Front of Norchen Dorje chang*

Material used: Brass

Height: 6"

Width: 3"

28. *Gonpo: Infront of Dogon chosgyal phagspa*

Material used: *Brass*

Height: 6"

Width: 3"

. To conclude, it is remarkable that the Lham Ḍas Khang is a well decorated Dukhang. The statues are well kept in glass almirah.

21

Thankas in Lham Das Khang

Lham Das Khang temple has many old and new Thankas, which are hanged through ceiling along the walls and with pole (Fig 21.1).

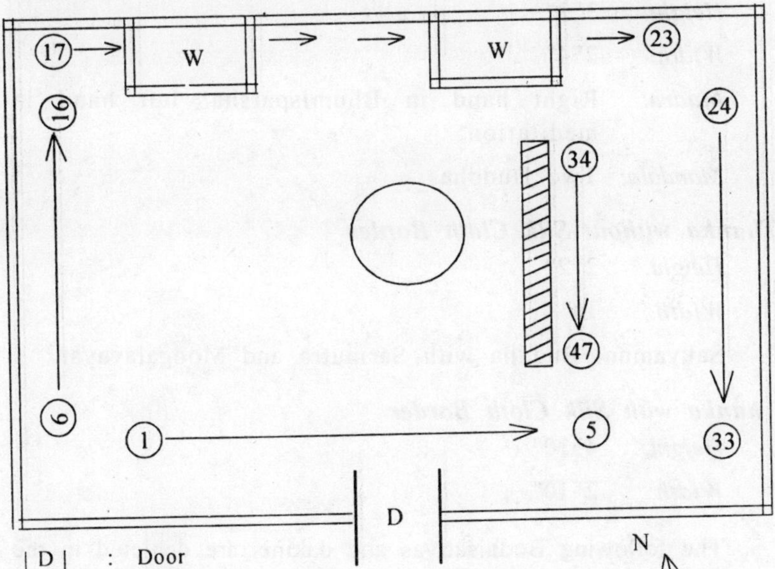

| D | : Door

○ : Pole

▨ : Beam

[W] : Window

| | : Wall

① to ㊼ : Thankas

Fig 21.1: Thankas in Lham Das Khang.

Above the Door Along the Wall from Right to Left

1. Avalokitesvara[1]

   Hands: Four

   Height: 3' 3"

   Width: 1' 3"

Thanka without Silk Cloth Border

   Height: 1'

   Width: 7'

2. Buddha

Thanka with Silk Cloth Border

   Height: 3' 2"

   Width: 2' 4"

   Mudra: Right hand in Bhumisparsha, left hand in meditation.

   Mandala: Two Buddhas

Thanka without Silk Cloth Border

   Height: 2' 2"

   Width: 10"

3. Sakyamuni Buddha with Sariputra and Modgalayayan[2]

Thanka with Silk Cloth Border

   Height: 4' 10"

   Width: 2' 10"

The following Bodhisattvas and dakinis are depicted in the mandala:

Upper to Centre Figure: At Centre

(i) Vajradhara[3]

Right to Vajradhara

(ii) Dogon chosgyal phagspa

(iii) Yogini khachotma

Left to the Vajradhara

(iv) Heyvajra (kydor)
(v) Four hands Avalokitasvara.

Below the Centre Figure: Right to Left

(vi) Dramje Zugchan[4]
(vii) Turdag (citipati)[5]
(viii) Two hands Gonpo[6]
(ix) Paldan Lhamo[7]

4. Amitayus [Long Life Buddha][8]
Position: Centre Figure: Left to Amitayus
(i) Dolkar

Right to Amitayus

(i) Namgyal ma

Upper Side of These Figures

(ii) Sachan Kunga nyingpo: Centre
(iii) Sonam Tsemo: Right to Centre
(iv) Sakya Pandita: Left to Centre

Left to Centre Sachan Kunga nyingpo

(v) Je tsun dakpa gyaltsen
(vi) Dogon chosgyal Phagspa

Below to Amitayus

(vii) Two hands Mahakala: Centre, wrathful.
(viii) Jungpo Dulcet: Wrathful, right to mahakala
(ix) Bhumi Devi: Next to Jungpo Dulcet.

Left to Mahakala

(x) Not identified

The above Amitayus thanka with silk cloth border has the following measurements:

Height: 8' 7"

Width: 7' 3"

Thanka without Silk Cloth Border

Height: 5' 8"

Width: 6'

5. Norchen Dorje Chan Kunga Zangpo[9]

Mudra: Right hand in Vitarka mudra, left hand rests near asana.

Symbols: Holds flower plant with Dorje and bell.

Thanka with Silk Cloth Border

Height: 5' 4"

Width: 3' 2"

Thanka without Silk Cloth Border

Height: 3' 1"

Width: 2' 2"

Behind the Buddhist statues at the lower shelf of the almirah, the following Thankas are hanged from right to left.

6. Dolma mandala:

Height: 4'

Width: 3' (Approx.)

7. TSEPAKMET (Amitayus): Surrounded with lamas and Bodhisattvas.

Mudra: Dhyana mudra with long life pot.

Height: 4' (with border cloth)

Width: 3' 6" (with border cloth)

8. Gyalva Lhachogs Singge:[10] Surrounded with lamas.

9. Sakyamuni Buddha with Sari putra and Modgalayayan.

Thanka with Silk Cloth

Height: 3'

Width: 2' (Approx.)

10. Avalokitesvara

Hands: Four, two main arms are in Namaskar mudra.

Mandala: Surrounded by lamas.

Thanka with Silk Cloth

Height: 4'

Width: 3' (Approx.).

11. Sachen Kungga Gyaltsen (Sakya Pandita)[11]

Mandala: Surrounded by Saskya lamas.

Thanka with Silk Cloth

Height: 4'

Width: 3' (Approx.)

12. Dogon Chosgyal Phagspa[12]

Mandala: Surrounded by lamas and other related deities.

Thanka with Silk Cloth Border

Height: 4'

Width: 3' (Approx.)

13. Vajradhara[13]

Mandala: Surrounded by Sakya liegn lamas

Thanka with Silk Cloth Border

Height: 4'

Width: 3' (Approx.)

14. Unidentified Deity

Symbol: Holds visvavajra

Thanka with Silk Cloth Border

Height 4'

Width: 3' (Approx.)

15. Dogon Chosgyal phagspa

Mandala: Buddha, White Tara and Bodhisattva

Thanka with Silk Cloth Border

Height: 3'

Width: 3' (Approx.)

16. Guru Padmasambhava (Guru Khamsum zilnon)[14]

Thanka with Silk Cloth Border

Height: 4'

Width: 3' (Approx.)

Thankas are Hanged Through Ceiling Along the Windows

17. A group of Vajra Kilas

Thanka with Silk Cloth Border

Height: 5' 4"

Width: 3' 6" (Approx.)

Thanka without Silk Cloth Border

Height: 3' 5"

Width: 2' 11"

18. White Mahakala[15]

Mandala: Surrounded by Sakya lamas and other related Bodhisattvas.

Thanka with Silk Cloth Border

Height: 4' 10"

Width: 3' 4"

Thanka without Silk Cloth Border

Height: 3' 4"

Width: 2' 9"

19. Guru Padmasambhava

Mandala: Avalokitesvara, Vajrapani, Amitayus, Boddhisattvas.

Thanka with Silk Cloth Border

Height: 5' 10"

Width: 3' 9"

20. Dolkar[16]

Thanka with Silk Cloth Border

Height: 3"

Width: 11'

Thanka without Silk Cloth Border

Height: 2' 2"

Width: 8"

21. Head of Sakya Tradition

Mandala: Surrounded by Buddha, Gonpo, Bodhisattvas

Thanka with Silk Cloth Border

Height: 4' 3"

Width: 2' 5" (without Silk Cloth Border)

Thanka without Silk Cloth Border

Height: 2' 10"

Width: 2' 5"

22. Guru Padmasambhava & Bodhisattva

Type of Thanka: Black

Thanka with Silk Cloth Border

Height: 4' 6"

Width: 3'

Thanka without Silk Cloth Border

Height: 2' 8"

Width: 2' 4"

23. Konkhen Gorampa Sodnam Singge[17]

Mundala: Surrounded by Buddha, Virupa, Sacian Kunga Nyingpo and Bodhisattvas

Thanka with Silk Cloth Border

Height: 5' 5"

Width: 3' 3"

Thanka without Silk Cloth Border

Height: 3' 10"

Width: 2' 4"

Towards Door Along the Wall

24. Unidentified Thanka

Condition: Bad

Thanka with Silk Cloth Border

Height: 4' 3"

Width: 2' 10"

Thanka without Silk Cloth Border

Height: 3'

Width: 2' (Approx.)

25. Unidentified Thanka

Condition: Very bad

Height: 4' 2" with silk cloth border

Width: 2' 11"

Thanka without Silk Cloth Border

Height: 2' 2"

Width: 2' 6"

26. Dolkar (Skt. White Tara)

Mandala: (i) Upper right Vajradhara

(ii) Below right Avalokitesvara

(iii) Upper left Milarepa

(iv) Below left Vajrasattva

Thanka with Silk Cloth Border

Height: 4' 5"

Width: 3'

Thanka without Silk Cloth Border

Height: 2' 9"

Width: 2' 2"

27. Manjusri[18]

Mudra: Seated

Hands: Two

Legs: Two

Head: One

Mandala: (i) Upper left Dorje chang

(ii) Upper right Sakya Pandita

(iii) Below left Green Tara

Height: 4' 3" with silk cloth border

Width: 3'

Thanka with Silk Cloth Border

Height: 2' 8"

Width: 2' 1"

29. Buddha?

Condition: Very Bad

Mandala: Chotpa lhamogyat, up four Buddhas in four directions.

Height: 4' 1" with silk cloth border

Width: 3' 4"

Thanka without Silk Cloth Border

Height: 2' 8"

Width: 2' 5"

30. Damcan Chosgyal?

Colour: Red

Thanka with Silk Cloth Border

Height: 4' 6"

Width: 3' 11"

Thanka without Silk Cloth Border

Height: 2' 10"

Width: 2' 2"

30. A lama with jewel

    Mudra and Symbol: Right hand preaching, left hand holds jewel.

Thanka with Silk Border

Height: 4'

Width: 2' 9" (without silk border)

Thanka without Silk Border

Height: 3' 3"

Width: 2' 9"

31. Yellow Tara[19]

    Mandala: Surrounded by Buddha and Bodhisattva

    Height: 4' with silk border

    Width: 2' 9"

Without Silk Border

Height: 2' 5"

Width: 11"

32. Avalokitesvara

    Posture: Standing

    Mandala: Dharmapalas

    Height: 3' 11" with silk border

    Width: 3' 4"

Thanka without Silk Border

Height: 2' 9"

Width: 2' 3"

33. Mahakala

    Thanka: Nagpo (black)

    Mandala: Wrathful Dharmapalas

    Hands: Two

Height: 4' 2"

Width: 2' 10"

Without Silk Border

Height: 2' 9"

Width: 2' 5"

Thankas Hanged with Ceiling Along Beams

Right to Left

34. Avalokitesvara

Hands: Four

Mudra: Two main arms in Namaskar mudra.

Height: 3' ·3" with silk border

Width: 1'

Without Silk Border

Height: 2' 2"

Width: 8"

35. Vajrapani[20]

Height: 3' 2" with silk border

Width: 2' 3"

Without Silk Border

Height: 2' 1"

Width: 1'

36. Unidentified

Condition: Very bad

Height: 2' 2" with silk border

Width: 2' 6"

Without Silk Border

Height: 2' 3"

Width: 2'

37. Six hands Gonpo[21]

Height: 2' 7" with silk border

Width: 1'

Without Silk Border

Height: 1'

Width: 6"

38. Two hands Gonpo

Colour: Black

Height: 3' with silk border

Width: 2' 2"

Without Silk Border

Height: 1'

Width: 6"

39. Unidentified

Height: 2' 10" with silk border

Width: 1'

Without Silk Border

Height: 1'

Width: 6"

40. Vajrapani

Height: 10" with silk border

Width: 6"

Without Silk Border

Height: 5"

Width: 4"

41. Unidentified

Height: 2' 10" with silk border

Width: 2' 4"

Without Silk border

Height: 8"

Width: 6"

42. Unidentified

Height: 2' 10" with silk border

Width: 1' 10"

Without Silk Border

Height: 1'

Width: 1'

43. Unidentified: A head lama of Sakya?

Height: 2' 9"

Width: 1'

With Silk Border

Height: 2' 4"

Width: 11"

44. Unidentified Mandala

Height: 2' 9" with silk border

Width: 2' 4"

Without Silk Border

Height: 1'

Width: 2' 3"

45. Unidentified Mandala

Height: 2' 9" with silk border

Width: 1'

Without Silk Border

Height: 1'

Width: 10"

46. Buddha Mandala

Height: 3' 2" with silk border

Width: 2' 2"

Without Silk Border

Height: 2' 1"

Width: 2"

47. Mandala?

Height: 3' 6" with silk border

Width: 2' 7"

Without Silk Border

Height: 2' 2".

Width: 2' 3"

This temple has H.H. Luding Khan Pinpoche's throne which is 7' in height and 4' 7" in width.

NOTES & REFERENCES

1. Avalokitesvara: Tib. Chenrezi. A Bodhisattva "The compassionate one." Sometimes is considered as one of the Dhyani Bodhisattvas, the creator and ruler of the present age.
2. Sakyamuni Buddha with Sariputra and Mudgalayayan: Tib. Shakya Tubpa; Pron. English, Tubpa "The Enlightened one" or "The Awakened one."

   Historically known as Goutama Buddha. He got enlightenment at Bodhgaya, later turned the three wheel of Dharma in Varanasi, Gradrakuta and Vaisali.
3. Vajradhara: Tib. Dorje chang. He is the Tantric manifestation of Sakyamuni Buddha. He has one calm face; two arms carries vajra and bell in Vajrahumukara mudra: Asana—Dhyana with dark-blue colour: wears—five leafed crown, carrying, fight necklace, armlet, wristlet, bracelet etc.
4. Dramje Zugchan: Tib rdramje—zugchan. Four face Mahakala. Yidam (Ishtdeva).
5. Turdag (citipati): A pair of dancing skeletons who are enemies

of thieves. Cf. Bruce, Fredrick W.: *An Encyclopaedia of Buddhist Deities, Demigods, Godlings, Saints and Demons,* D.K. Print World, New Delhi, Vol. I, 1994: 107.

6. Two hands Gonpo: The universal protector in Sanskrit equivalent to Mahakala an emanation of the Pancha-Buddha. A Dharmapala, as a wrathful god he destroys the enemies of Buddhist teachings.
7. Padan Lhamo: Tib. Dpal ldan lha mo, "The Glorious Goddess," is one of the most important protectors of the Geluk pa tradition of Mahayana Buddhism. She was initiated by Chagna Dorje and was given the name Dorje Naljorma.
8. Amitayus: He is the Buddha of longevity; generally shown in meditation mudra, an urn resting on his palms, which contains pills of longevity. In Sambhogakaya he appears in the form of Dhyani Buddha named Amitabha. According to the Mahayana Buddhist tradition he is shown in golden/red colour.
9. Norchen Dorje Chan Kunga Zangpo: Sakya lama of Mahayana Buddhism.
10. Gyalva Lhachogs Singge: A Lama of Mahayana Buddhism.
11. Sachen Kungga Gyaltsen (Sakya Pandita): He was the great scholar lama of Sakya tradition of Mahayana Buddhism.
12. Dogon Chosgyal Phagspa: Head lama of Sakya order and great scholar of Sakya tradition of Mahayana Buddhism.
13. Vajradhara: Tib. Dorje Chang. He is the tantric manifestation of Sakyamuni Buddha has one calm face, two arms carries vajra and bell in Vajrahumkara mudra. Cf. Bunce, Fredrick W.: *'An Encyclopaedia of Buddhist Deities, Demgods, Godlings, Saints and Demons,'* Vol. I, D.K. Prinworld Ltd., New Delhi, 1994: 577.
14. Guru Padmasambhava (Guru khamsum zilnon): An Indian teacher/guru who spread tantric Buddhism through Tibet, during eighth century A.D. One of the eighty four Mahasiddhas, saints and miracle workers, sometimes known as the eighty four great sorcerers.
15. White Mahakala: Tib Gonkar. A Dharmapal, a deity who has wrathful form and considered a god who destroys the enemies of Buddhist teachings. He is depicted in white colour.
16. Dolkar: She is one of the form of Dolma or Tara. It is believed that by worshipping Tara, one may get liberation from this *samsara.* She is depicted in various forms viz. White Tara, Blue Tara, Green Tara, Red Tara, Yellow Tara etc. Dolkar is white form of Tara.

17. Konkhen Gorampa Sodnam Singge: A scholar lama of Sakya tradition of Mahayana Buddhism.
18. Manjusri: He is the embodiment of the wisdom of all the Buddhas, and purposefully descended to the world as a Bodhisattva for the welfare of all sentient beings. Buddhists believe that he is the sole deity of wisdom.
19. Yellow Tara: She is one of the form of Tara and is regarded as the manifestation of Avalokitesvara, normally belongs to the deity of action tantra and specially worshipped in Buddhism as the bestower of life protector.
20. Vajrapani: Tib. Phyag-na-rdo-rje-tho-drug-pa; Pron. Eng. Phyag dor, One of a traid of mountain deities known as rigs-gsum-mgon-po, and includes: spyan-res-gzigz and jam-dpal-dbyangs.
21. Six hands Gonpo. Tib. Mgon po phyag drug pa, myur mdzad-ye-shes-kyi-mgon-po-phyag-drug-pa. In Sanskrit equivalent of Sadhbuja Mahakala. One of the Dharmapala images. He has one face, three eyes, fierce, flame like-hair; Six arms; body corpulent, legs two; colour Dark blue or black and vahana: prostrate human. He is the wrathful manifestation of Avalokitesvara. Cf. Bunce, Fredrick W.: *An Encyclopaedia of Buddhist Deities, Demigods, Godlings, Saints and Demons, op. cit.*, 1994: 464.

22

Statues in Lhakhang Yu Lo Khang (Lha Khang Gyu Lo Bkhang)

The Lhakhang does not have many statues like others have. It has some Dolma Statues. Details are furnished hereafter.

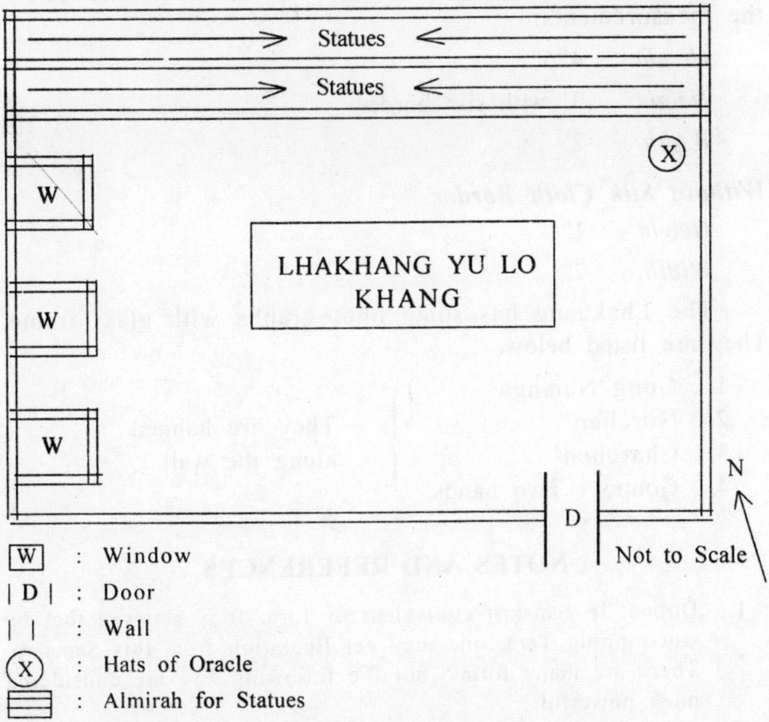

Fig. 22.1: Statues in Lhakhang Yu Lo Khang.

Statue of the Lhakhang

Dolma[1] [In the Almirah]

Height:	4' 5"	main statute
Width:	3'	

Statues in the Almirah

On the left up of the Centre are five Dolmas. On the right up also are five Dolmas. Similarly at the down left and right of the Centre statue has five Dolmas each, with Height 2' 3" and width 10".

This Lhakhang also called Dolma Lhakhang, there are four pairs (or eight hats of oracle). Besides twenty one small Dolma Thankas are hanged along the ceiling with the beam. Here follows the measurements:

Height: 4' 5"

Height: 3' with silk border

Width: 2'

Without Silk Cloth Border

Height: 1'

Width: 7"

The Lhakhang has some photographs with glass frame. They are listed below:

1. Gong Namnga[2]
2. Norchen[3]
3. Charchen[4]
4. Gonpo: [5] Two hands

} They are hanged along the wall.

NOTES AND REFERENCES

1. Dolma: In Sanskrit equivalent to Tara. It is believed that by worshipping Tara, one may get liberation from this Samsara. There are many forms. but the following five are considered most powerful:

   (i) The White Tara

   (ii) The Green Tara

(iii) The Red Tara

(iv) The Blue Tara

(v) The Yellow Tara

Cf. Finegan, Jack: *Tibet: A Dreamt of Image,* Tibet House, New Delhi; 1986: 135.

2. Gongma Namnga: Five great Sakya lamas viz. Sachen Kunga Nyingpo, Sonam Tsemo, Dakpa Gyaltsan, Sakya Pandia and Drogon Chosgyal Phagspa.
3. Norchen: Tib. Ngorchen Kunga Zangpo (1382-1457). A famous lama of Sakya tradition.
4. Charchen: Tib. Tsarchen Losal Gyatso (1502- '56) a famous lama of Tsar lineage of Sakya Tradition.
5. Gonpo: Two hands: Gonpo is the wrathful manifestation of Avalokitesvara. The following story goes about the Gonpo: "One day Nagarjuna, the Abbot of Nalanda monastery, was working at his garden along with his monk students. Dharma protector then miraclely turned into a self-emanated image by the side of a nearby river. When Nagarjuna came near the image, he found that the image turned with one face and two arms. He offered ritual cake. Then image turned to his real form of Dharma protector. Cf. Ladrang Kalsang: *'The Guardian Deities of Tibet,'* Little Lhasa Pub. Dharamsala, H.P. 2000: 37.

23

Paintings in Lakcung Temple

There is no big statues in this temple, however, there are many beautiful paintings (Fig 23.1)

The frescos of this temple was made under the direction of

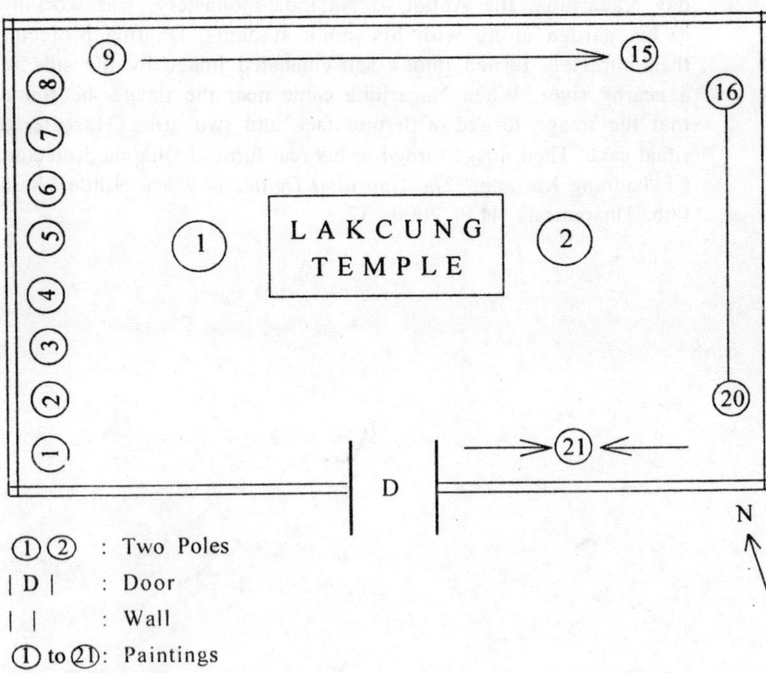

Fig. 23.1: Paintings in Lakcung Temple.

Lama Tungpa Dorje, the founder of the monastery. Here follows the details:

1. Kurgon (Tib. Gur-gyi-mgon-po) [1]

   Hands: Two

   Height: 5'

   Width: 4' 4"

2. Lama

   Height: 2' 11"

   Width: 2' 4"

3. Buddha Amitabha: [2]

   Height: 4' 11"

   Width: 4' 3"

4. A Lama: [The fresco damaged by rain water]

   Height: 3'

   Width: 2' 8"

5. Buddha: [New painting]

   Height: 4' 8"

   Width: 4' 3"

6. Sachan Kunga Nying po: [3]

   Height: 3' 7"

   Width: 2' 10"

7. Buddha: [4]

   Mudra: Left hand in Dhyana mudra with jewel. Right hand in preaching.

   Height: 4' 11"

   Width: 3' 10"

8. A head lama of Sakya tradition.

   Height: 2' 10"

   Width: 2' 5"

Paintings on the Wall in Front of the Door

9. Kha spyod ma (Tib. Mkh'a spyod ma):[5]

Depiction: Shown nude

Asana: Stepping to Right

Symbols: Karttrka, Kapala and Khatvanga

Special forms: Drinks blood from a kapala held in the left hand, right holds karttrka, khatvanga hangs over left shoulder. Visvavajra is in the Usnisa.

Ornaments: Human skulls garland; Other like Dharmapala ornaments.

10. Unidentified:

Mudra: Vajrahumkara; right hand holds vajra, rests near breast. Left hand with bell.

Height: 4' 4"

Width: 3' 6"

11. Unidentified (Probably Vajradhara):[6]

Mudra: Vajrahumkara; wrists crossed at breast, holding vajra and ghanta.

Body: Black-Blue

Asana: Dhyana

Ornaments: Bodhisattva

Height: 3'

Width: 2' 6"

12. Sakyamuni Buddha with his main disciples: Sariputra and Modgalayayana.[7]

Buddha

Height: 4' 6"

Width: 3' 8"

The measurements of Sariputra and Modgalayayana are:

Height: 3' 6"

Width: 8"

13. Unidentified:

    Mudra: Right hand holds *Digug* with symbols Vajra perpendicular to earth. Left hand holds skull cup near breast.

    Posture: Sitting with wrathful form

    Height: 2' 8"

    Width: 2' 8"

14. Amitayus[8]

    Mudra: Dhayana with pot

    Height: 4' 6"

    Width: 3' 6"

15. Guru Padmasambhava[9]

    Posture: Seated

    Height: 3' 2"

    Width: 2' 7"

Painting on the Left Side Wall of the Door

16. Buddha:

    Mudra: Preaching

    Height: 4' 11"

    Width: 4' 2"

17. Birupa:[10]

    Body: Brown

    Height: 3' 5"

    Width: 2' 5"

    Posture: Seated

18. Buddha

    Mudra: Dhyana

    Height: 5'

    Width: 4'

19. Sakya Pandita[11]

    Height: 3' 6"

    Width: 2' 11"

20. Sakyamuni Buddha

Condition of Painting: New

Mudra: Right hand in Bhumisparsha. Left in Dhyana

Height: 4' 7"

Width: 4' 3"

Paintings along the Wall Left Side of the Door

21. Namtosras:

Symbol: Holds Nakula omits jewels.

Height: 5'

Width: 4' 5"

NOTES AND REFERENCES

1. Kurgon: Tib. Gur-gyi-mgon-po-lha-brgyad, bstan-srung-kun-gyi=sde-dpon-rdo-rje-gur, rdo-rje-nag-po-chen-po. In Sanskrit equivalent 'Panjara Mahakala. Cf. Bunce, Fredrick W.: *An Encyclopaedia of Buddhist Deities, Demigods, Godlings, Saints and Demons,* D.K. Pub., Delhi, 389.
2. Buddha Amitabha: He is the Buddha of Infinite light, is known as the fourth of the Dhyani Buddha. He resides in Sukhavai, in the Western quarter of heaven. Cf. Sanjib Kumar Das: *'Tara: An Exhibition of rare Buddhist Thankas,'* CIBS, Leh-Ladakh, 2003: 20.
3. Sachan Kung a Nying po: Sakya lama of Mahayana order of Buddhism.
4. Buddha: In other words Lord Sakyamuni Buddha. He practiced all kinds of Bodhisattva's activities for countless acons to attain perfect enlightenment. He delivered religious sermons for the benefit of all sentient beings. Cf. Lobzang Tsewang *Sakyamuni: An Exhibition of Rare Thankas,* CIBS, Leh-Ladakh, 2001: 20.
5. Kha spyod ma (Tib. mkh'a spyod ma): Yidam or personal protective deity.
6. Vajradhara: He is the tantric manifestation of Sakyamuni Buddha, and has one calm face, two arms carries vajra and bell in Vajrahumkara mudra Cf. Bunce, Fredrick W.: *'An Encyclopaedia of Buddhist Deities, Demigods, Godlings, Saints and Demons,'* Vol. I, D.K. Printworld Ltd., New Delhi, 1994: 577.
7. Buddha Sakyamuni with his main disciples Sariputra and

Modgalayayana: In 6th Century B.C. Buddha Sakyamuni descended to the world to show the right path to the fortunate beings, so that they may attain freedom from the cycle of existence. He practiced all kinds of Bodhisattva's activities for countless acons to attain perfect enlightenment. He delivered religious sermons for the benefit of all sentient beings traveling from one place to another till the end of his life. Cf. Lobzang Tsewang; *op. cit.*: 20.

8. Amitayus: Also known as Buddha Amitayu or Buddha of longevity. In Sambhogakaya he is appeared in the form of Bhyani Buddha and mostly represents in golden colour in the meditation mudra carries an urn on his palms, which contains pills of longevity. He wears robes and various ornaments. As a lord of Buddha longevity he is widely worshipped by Buddhists of Himalayan regions.
9. Guru Padmasambhava: He was the great mystic saint from India who had tremendous miraculous powers. He brought Buddhist Tantra in Tibet in the 8th century A.D. and introduced its learning and practice. He is venerated by all Tibetans as the second Buddha. He subdued the local deities and demons who were obstructing the construction of Samyas monastery. Cf. Lobzang Tsewang; *op. cit.*, 26.
10. Birupa: In Sanskrit equivalent Virupa, a Mahasiddha.
11. Sakya Pandita: In Tibetan language he is equivalent kun dgra' rgyal mtshan (kunga Gyentsen). He was born in 1182 A.D. Later became abbot of Sakya, attained reputation in Buddhist philosophy, and was popularly known as Sa-kya Pandita meaning "The learned Sakya order." Cf. Finegan, Jack: *Tibet: A Dreamt of Image*, Tibet House, New Delhi, 1986: 105.

24

Thankas in Lakung Temple

The temple is also decorated with thanka painting which is a scroll painting and has many forms such as:

(1) Dhyani Buddhas:[1]
- (a) Vairocana
- (b) Aksobhya
- (c) Rotnasambhava
- (d) Amitabha
- (e) Amoghasiddhi

(2) Dhyani Bodhisattvas:[2]
- (a) Samantabhadra
- (b) Vajrapani
- (c) Ratnapani
- (d) Avalokitesvara
- (e) Visvapani

(3) Manusi Buddhas:[3]
- (a) Krakucchanda
- (b) Kanakamuni
- (c) Kasyapa
- (d) Sakyamuni
- (e) Maitreya

(4) Taras:[4]
- (a) Sitatara (White Tara)
- (b) Syamatara (Green Tara)
- (c) Bhrkuti (Yellow Tara)
- (d) Ekjajata (Blue Tara)
- (e) Kurukalla (Red Tara)

(5) Yi-Dam[5] (Tutelary Gods):
(a) Hevajra
(b) Sang-dui
(c) Mahamaya
(d) Jambhala
(e) Kalacakra
(f) Yab-yum forms of Dhyanibuddhas

(6) Dharmapala[6]
(a) Sridevi
(b) Brahma
(c) Beg-tse
(d) Yama
(e) Kubera
(f) Mahakala
(g) Hayagriva (or Heygriva)
(h) Yamantaka

(7) Minor Gods:[7]
(a) Vaisravana
(b) Virudhaka
(c) Dhritarastra
(d) Virupaksa

(8) Mahapancaraja:[8]
(a) Bi-har (Pe-har)
(b) Chos-skyon
(c) Kuirgyal po
(d) Sung-girgyal-po
(e) Yon-tan rgyal-po

(9) Mahasiddhas:[9] Eighty four great sorcerers

(10) Non- human types[10]
(a) Citipati
(b) Nagas
(c) Garudas
(d) Demons
(e) Witches

(11) Historical Personages Deifed:[11]

(a) Disciples of Gautama
(b) Sixteen Arhats
(c) Nagarjuna
(d) Padmasambhava
(e) Atisa
(f) Mi-la re-pa
(g) Tsong-kha-pa
(h) Dharmaraja
(i) Dalai lamas
(j) Lamas of the related traditions.

In this temple some of the Thankas can be identified based according to the above said Buddha, Bodhisattvas etc. Here follows the details:

(1) Kongma Namnga:[12]

Position: Centre figure

Mandala: Birupa, Dorje chang, Hevajra, Gonpo Dandi, Ngorchen Kunga zang po, Tser chen choskyi Lodos.

Thanka with Silk Border

Height: 4' 5"

Width: 2'

(2) Medicine Buddha[13]

Nature:Painted on hard paper upper to Medicine Buddha Panchen chogla namgyal

Position: Centre

Right and Left to centre, figures are not identified

Below to the Centre figure right side chostak, in the middle Sakya thuba and left side unidentified.

Thanka with Silk Border

Height: 3'

Width: 2' 5"

3. Gonpo Dandi:[14]

Mandala: Dharmapalas, Bodhisattvas and lamas of Sakya tradition.

Thanka with silk border

Height: 5'

Width: 3' 10"

Thanka without Silk Border

Height: 3' 2"

Width: 2' 7"

(4) Gonpa Dandi:

Mandala: Upper right to left of the centre figure are:

(i) Four hands Gonpo
(ii) Head lama of Sakya order
(iii) Unidentified
(iv) Padam Lhamo
(v) Unidentified
(vi) Citipati
(vii) Damzug

Thanka with Silk Cloth Border

Height: 5' 4"

Width: 4'

Tanka without Silk Border

Height: 3'8"

Width: 3' 10"

The above thanka is old but has new silk cloth border.

5. Manjusri:[15]

Thanka does not have silk cloth border, has following measurements:

Height: 2' 7"

Width: 2' 3"

NOTES AND REFERENCES

1. Godeon, Antoinette K: *The Iconography of Tibetan Lamaism*, Munshiram Manoharlal, Pub. Ltd., 1998: 31.
2. *Ibid.*, 32.
3. *Ibid.*
4. *Ibid.*, 34
5. *Ibid.*, 36
6. *Ibid.*
7. *Ibid.*, 37
8. *Ibid.*
9. *Ibid.*
10. *Ibid.*, 32.
11. *Ibid.*, 38
12. Kongma Namnga
13. Medicine Buddha Sangye Menlha, in Sanskrit equivalent to Baisajyaguru. The Medicine Buddha is the Buddha of healing, who is invoked to care for the sick. He wears the monastic robes of a Buddha and sits on lotus blossom upon a lion throne. His body is dark blue. Cf. Bunce, Fredric W.: *An Encyclopaedia of Buddhist Deities, Demigods, Godlings, Saints and Demons,'* Vol. I, D.K. Printworld Ltd., New Delhi, 1994: 338.
14. Gonpo Dandi: Tib mGon po beng in Sanskrit equivant to Danda Mahakala. A Dharmapala. He is depicted in the following way. Face: One, fierce, three eyes; Arms: Two – Right hand holds Dorje, left hand holds skull cup; a stick rest on his hands across his body; body : Lion skin; standing on human corpse; Asana: Alidhasana, Colour: Blue; Vahana: Human corpse. Cf. Bunce, Fredric W.; *op. cit.*, New Delhi; 1994:114.
15. Manjusri: In Tibetan equivalent to Jam dbyangs, Pron. Jamyang "Charming Splendor," and is shown is yellow, white, red, blue and black forms; beautifully handsome young Mahabodhisattva and god of wisdom, science and agriculture. He is considered by the Northern Buddhists as one of the eight Dhyani Bodhisattvas. Cf. Bunce, Fredric W.; *op cit.*, New Delhi; 1994: 331.

    Note: The temple has one thanka at the gap above the hard paper painting. It is Namtosras:

    Height: 2' 9"
    Width: 2' 3"

25

Small Buddhist Statues in Lakung Temple

It is significant to note that Lakung temple is not in a good condition which needs immediate renovative measures for upkeep. It has some small statues and one stone carving. Here follows details:

1. Buddha[1]
2. Lama, Sakya tradition
3. Lama of Sakya order
4. Avalokitesvara[2]
5. Unidentified

   Symbols: Holds sun and moon.
6. Lama

Stone Carvings

(1) Avalokitesvara:[3]

Hands: Six

Mudra: Latitasana; left leg pendant, right leg in usual position of a Buddha.

Height: 3' 2"

Width: 2'

Besides it has one statue: Vajrapani[4]

Height: 3'

Width: 2' 8"

NOTES AND REFERENCES

1. *Buddha:* He descended to the earth to show the right path to the fortunate beings, so that they may attain eternal freedom from the cycle of life. He practised all kinds of Bodhisattva's activities for countless acons to attain perfect enlightenment. He delivered religious sermons for the benefit of all sentient beings travelling from one place to another till the end of his life. The Prajnaparamita is the central teaching of Lord Buddha. Cf. Lobzang Tsewang: *'Sakyamuni: An Exhibition of Rare Thankas,'* C.I.B.S. Leh-Ladakh; 2001: 20
2. *Avalokitesvara:* He is the Buddha of compassion and is a manifestation of the Buddha in the enjoyment body. In cross legged sitting posture is considered the Bodhisattva of kindness and compassion. The four handed Avalokitesvara hold jewels in their central pair, the second right hand a rosary and second left a white lotus. The body colour is white. Om Mani Padme Hum is his mantra. The recitation of his mantra purifies mind, body and speech. Cf. Sanjib Kumar Das: *Tara,* CIBS, Leh, 2003: 26.
3. *Avalokitesvara:* Tib Chanrazi, chak-zhi-pa "The compassionate one," literally: A Mahabodhisattva and one of the most popular Bodhisattvas in the world of Buddhism. The Fourth Dhyani Bodhisattva, the creator and ruler of the present age, an emanation of Dhyani Buddha Amitabha, who was born from a shining white ray of light which sprang from meditation. Cf. Bunce, Fredrick W. : *'An Encyclopaedia of Buddhist Deities, Demigods, Godlings, Saints and Demons,'* Volume-I, D.K. Printworld Limited, New Delhi; 1994: 36.
4. *Vajrapani:* Tib. Phyag-na-rdo-rje-tho-drug-pa, Pron. Eng. Phyag-dor. One of a triad of mountain deities known as rigs-gsum-mgon-po - and includes: spyan-ras-gzigz- and 'jam-dpal-dbyangs. He is the Bodhisattva of energy and power. During peaceful aspect, he is represented as a blue Bodhisattva holding a lotus; has one face, fierce, three eyes, flame like hair, two hands holds thunderbolt in his right hand and left hand is placed before his heart. He is the emanation and spiritual son of the Dhyani Buddha Aksobhya and the protector of Nagas and may assume a garuda form in this role. Cf. Bunce, Fredric W.: *'An Encyclopaedia of Buddhist Deities, Demigods, Godlings, Saints and Demons,'* Vol. I. D.K. Print World Pvt. Ltd., New Delhi; 1994: 397.

26

Matho Festival

Matho festival (Tib. Mang tro Nagrang) is celebrated in Matho monastery every year on the 14th and 15th days of the Ist Tibetan month. During the festival concerned monks perform Tantric dances and two gods known Rong-tsan made their special appearance. In fact, festival preparation starts one week earlier. During this period, besides cham practice, Lamas of the monastery use to make Mandala and offer prayers.

On the 14th of the 1st Tibetan month the following Dharmapala perform cham:

1. Gurgi Gonpo (Tib. gur gyi mgon po)[1]
2. akajati (Tib. ae Kadzati)[2]
3. Paldan Chamo dodkham vang chuk ma (Tib dpal ldan lha mo 'a dod kham phyug ma)[3]
4. Nagmo not chin (Tib. neg mo gnod soyin)
5. Puta (Tib. pu tra)[4]
6. Bata (Tib. bta ta)[5]
7. Singmo ral cik ma (Tib. sring mo ral gcig ma).[6]

Before the beginning of cham, two lamas dress up with old man and women costumes, and perform dance at the chamra for public entertainment. After the completion of above dance, the following cham comes one by one.

1. Zanak Cham (Tib. **Zhva Nag Cham)**

In this cham lamas after wearing zanak masks and costumes, come at the chamra and perform the same after offering Serkyams (Tib. rskyems).

2. Pumet Cham (Tib. **Bu Dmed Cham)**

In olden days on an average 100 pumet used to dance with Gonpo as helpers. Today as a symbol and some young lamas after wearing masks perform cham with Gonpo. All of them beat drums during cham. The name of the cham is derived from the Pumet as Pumet cham.

3. Kespe Cham (Tib. **Skyes P'al Cham)**

In olden days about one hundred helpers perform cham. Nowadays as their symbol some lamas after wearing masks and costumes perform cham alongwith Gonpo. Normally five lamas after wearing different masks and lama dress perform cham with Gonpo. During Cham they beat drums.

4. Dagspe Cham (Tib. **Sdags 'Jai Cham)**

In this, some lamas after wearing masks and costumes perform cham at chamra alongwith Goñpo.

5. Lhaskyi Gonpo (Tib. **Las Kyi Mgon Po)**

Lamas after wearing masks of puta-Bata Singmo ralcikma perform cham at the chamra.

6. Gonpo Zalzee Pa[7] (Tib. Mgon Po Zhal Bzhi Pa)

Lamas during this cham wear Gonpo gur nagpo, Norcin and Nagmo Norcin Paldan Lhamo masks, and perform the same in various ways at the chamra.

7. Chamzok

This is lunch break.

All the lamas who participate in the cham take rest for lunch.

8. Turdag Cham[8] (Tib. **Tur Bdag Cham)**

On this occasion two lamas wear turdak masks & costumes and perform cham at the chamra.

9. Group Cham

This time all the earlier Deities who had performed cham, once again come together in group alongwith two Lhas and perform cham.

10. Lhaskyi Gonpo Cham

This time two Matho Lhas dance alongwith gonpos. At the end two Gonpos cut 'Davo' (enemy).

11. Shava Cham

Thereafter two lamas with shava[9] (deer) masks come to chamra and perform cham. The deer is the symbol of compassion. The Shawas while dancing pray that wisdom and compassion should be released into the world and all earthly delusions should vanish.

At the end of the day musicians come to the chamra with their musical instruments viz. Daman and Surna. They play music. This time two Matho Lhas enter into the Gonkhang, then run along the roofs of Matho monastery. As they stop, people gathered there and starting to ask their future.

NOTES AND REFERENCES

1. Gurgi Gonpo (Tib. gur gyi mgon po): It is said that when Buddha was preaching on 'Dorje Gurgi gyud' (Tib. rpo-rje'ai gur gyi rgyud), one secret letter 'Hum' suddenly came out from his 'citta.' Thereafter he was known as Gurgi gonpo. Normally he has two hands. Buddhist pray him as '*Idam*' He is the Dharma Protector Cf. Jamyang Gyaltsen (ed.): *The History of Ladakh Monasteries,* 1995: 459.
2. Ikajati (Tib. ae kadzati): He is the protector of Buddha and Bodhisattvas. Besides, is known as a Dharma protector. Cf. Jamyajng Gyaltsen, *op. cit.*
3. Paldan Lhamo dodkham vangchukma (Tib. dpal ldan lha mo 'adod kham phyug ma): She is the Tantric deity and the main protector of Geluk pa order of Mahayana Buddhism. However, in the form of 'vangchukma' she is known as a daughter of Shiva. Cf. Jamyang Gyaltsan, *op. cit.*
4. Puta (Tib. pu tra): She is the protector of Padmasambhava's Dharma.
5. Bata (Tib. bta ta): He is also the protector of Nyingma pa order of Buddhism as founded by Padmasambhava.
6. Singmo ral cik ma (Tib. sring mo ral gcigma) : She is the protector of Padmasambhava's Dharma in Tibet.
7. Gonpo zal zee pa (Tib. mgon po zhal bzhi pa): This Gonpo has

many forms: In Matho monastery the following forms of Gonpos are worshipped:

(i) Ferocious face at the centre

(ii) Ferocious two faces blue colour

(iii) Left and Right green colour ferocious four faces; four hands. He is the ferocious form of Avalokitesvara and the main protector of the Sakya order of Buddhism.

8. Turdag cham: There are two skeleton statues of Turdak in Gnkhang. They are the Dharmapalas, during Nagrang perform tantric dance. Turdaks are graveyard protector spirits, who represent impermanence and encourage non-attachmrnt to ones physical bodies which is the only way a practitioner can escape the wheel of life.

9. *Shava:* During annual gonpa festival, two lamas, dressed in yellow hats (Tib. rtsedza) and rich silk garments welcome the deer by playing music on the Gyaling. This is a special flute that can only be played by the Lamas. The deer is the symbol of compassion and it prays that wisdom and compassion should be released into the world and all earthly delusions should be removed. They are the chhatrapalas and protect the Buddha Dharma.

27

Annual Prayer Time Table of the Monastery

1. 8th of the second month of Tibetan Calender two Matho lhas offer prayer at the Dok Pug.
2. 13th of the same month lamas of the monastery read Kangyur (Tib. k'a 'agyur rin poche) *pothi* for three days.
3. 8th of the 4th month of Tibetan calendar lama prayer stong chost (Tib. stong mchot). On this occasion they offer one thousand *chog* and lit lamps.
4. 15th of the 4th month of the Tibetan calender lamas of the monastery perform Buddha's parinirvana day and offer prayer by making one hundred *chog* (Tib. tsogs).
5. 4th of the 5th month of the Tibetan calender lamas of the monastery offer *Chotpa* (mcho pa) to Sakya Pandita and Tsongkhapa Thankas and prayer Dolma yunclock (sgrol ma yul mdos).
6. 4th of the 6th Tibetan month lamas and people of Matho remember Buddha teachings and carry *pothis* of Buddha teaching around the monastery. People take fast and worship Buddha.
7. 25-29 of the 9th Tibetan month Lamas offer Jigjet prayer, later throw *bela* (torma) outside of the village. Before throwing out *torma* lamas offer prayer to the concerned deity in the dark room.
8. 12th of 10th Tibetan calendar month lamas of the monastery offer kangrol (Tib. bskang-gso) prayer in the Gonkhang.
9. Lostor: 12-20 of 10th month Lamas by new Lastor offer

prayer. The morning and evening prayer is called stor bun (Tib. gtor-'abul).

10. 15th of the 10th Tibetan month lamas select persons for lhas. On the above day lamas of the monastery gather in the monastery. Comner offer lhacan god prayer on 3, 8, 15, day of the month.
11. 24th of the 10th Tibetan month lamas perform Gustor according the Nyingma tradition.
12. 15th of 3rd month lamas offer prayer khangcan dorjechan khadup gyatso (Tib. khan chen rdo-rje 'achang mkhas grub rgya mtso) and Trongkhapa lamchot prayer.
13. 29th of 3rd month offer prayer to Khangchen Dorjechan Jamyang gyaltsen spal zangpo (Tib. Khan-Chen rdo-rje 'achang 'ajan-dbyangs rgyal mtsan dpal bzangpo).
14. 25th of 4th month offer prayer to Dochen Dorje chang kunga zangpo (Tib. dor chen rdo-rje 'achang kun dg'a bzang po).
15. 15th of 7th Tibetan month offer prayer to Dulva zee zicum (Tib. 'dul ba gzhi gsum).
16. Lamas go for 15 days yarnas (Tib. dbyar gnas) in 1st month.
17. 1st of 8th month lamas celebrate Sozong (Tib. so so'ai). On this day lamas take relief from the promise which they had taken that not to do any kind of sin.
18. 14 of 9th month lamas offer prayer for kunga Ningbo Sakya lama (Tib. Kun dg'a snying po).
19. 22th of 9 month gonpa celebrate Tushitavatar divas. On this day Buddha again appeare on earth from Tushitloka (heaven).
20. 14th of 11th month lamas of the monastery offer prayer to Sakya Pandita.

In nutshell, we can summarized the calender events in the following way (Table 27.1).

TABLE 27.1

Events in the Matho Monastery According to the Tibetan Calendar

Month	*Day*	*Events*
(1)	(2)	(3)
2nd	13-15	Reading of Kangyur
4th	8-10	Worship of goddess Vijaya, special prayer service to Buddha and Ghanchakra
5th	08	Prayers to the greatest scholars of Sakya Kunga Gyaltsan and display his Thanka.
6th	04	Dharmacakra Parvartan day
6th	15	'Varshavas' for monks for 45 days
9th	25-28	Vajra Bhairava prayer
10th	12-20	Worship tutelary deities
11th	14	Death ceremony of Kunga Gyaltsan

28

Tibetan Inscription in the Lhun Grub Khang

TEXT

sva sti bi jo yantu/
sdon dus mh'a ci ni'ai yul gru na/
bskal pa chags p'ai thog ma byung b'ai grag/
tho mdzes nlung gi dpen gnas nyams dg'a ru/
'achi met dgon po grub p'ai drang srod byung/
de mthus brag ni deyi 'agram pa nas/
rga shi med p'ai bcud len che yi chu/
rtag par 'abab cir mya ngan p'ai shing/
me tog 'abras bus la shig kyang bkyes/
drang srong de'ai byams p'ai na bna/
zang zing mi 'ajigs sbyin p'ai gyab mos/
'akhor 'abas p'a 'arab chags sbu sdug tang/
ri dgas nu dang nas p'ang tse ring gyur/
de dag sbangs pa bde ba la/
neg pa gang phyin tsering rnam drug ces/
grags p'ai gr'a prin yig phyogs bya kya dg'a ma yi/
mkhur chas rnams par mdzes p'ai rgyan ru dbyin/
dpag yas bsod nams mams bsgyed p'ai
rnam pa thams cad mkhyen p'ai gzugs sku la/
jegs par mng'a b'ai bkra shes rtags brgyad kyi/
bzugs nyan dpang gzhugs gsar p'ai lang cho can/
'adi dga gang gi khyim du 'adra byed na/

'achi med tse dang na ba med pa bed/
rga dang rgud pa med lang tso stobs/
mi zang basod na nams pung po'ai 'aphel 'agyur/
phyi dang nang gi mthun pa min p'ae phyogs/
'ajoms p'ai gyen po mchog kyang 'adi len zhes/
chos kun rcen cing "abrel ban 'abyung p'ai 'aprul/
shes nas sma ba mang pos mchen du gling/
dge lags shes p'ai mchon ni sa mig gi dpyid/
bkod p'ai rten 'abyung dge bas mg'a mham gyi/
lus can tse yi lon shing rgyas p'ai khrod/
sed bzhi 'ai 'abras du gyur du zabar shog/
de dag ma srun sgyod pa nid snagas nas/
byams p'ai 'adzum mdangs dkar pos bsu bzhin du/
bed dang dge b'ai bdud ci rcag 'athung p'ai/
bkra shis deam p'ai sa stengs brbyen gyuyr cig/
te ltar gnas khang gang da bkra shis
'ai rten 'abrel du/
'adri bar 'aos b'ai tse ring rnam la drug dang/
bkra shis rtags brgyad kyi gzags
brhan rnam par bgod pa la/
nye bar mkho bar ba shar pa chigs su bcang ba/
adi yang sgro btags smra ba bnde
tsul khrims rin chen gyis/
dpal sde ge lhun grub
sto chos grar bris pa 'ao
mang lam/ bkra shis
- -
- -
nang gzhan legs lam 'agod pa smod lam/
- - - - - - - - - - - - - - / gnga lam gsum rgyu
yang nyes skyod dam/
ri bsil -
sbyod b'ai zil ming byed/

K'a shi li yul bdag rgyal pos bsru ngas p'ai phyogs/
nags tsal srhag po zhig tu glang chen sprel/
ri bong gong ma sred de srog chags p'ai/
byung ba pan tshun yid gcugs mdz'a par gnas/

ROMAN TRANSLITERATION

ova sti bi jo yontu/
don tus maha cine yul du na/
kalpa chags pe thog ma jung ve dag/
tho zes lungi pen nas nyam ga ru/
chimet gonpo dub pe drang sod jung/
de thuk dagri te ye dam pa nas/
ga shi met pe cur len che ye chu/
tak par bab cing nyang pe sing/
men tok dasbu zi va zig kyang kes/
tang song teyi cams pe na ban/
zang zing ming zig cin pe yab mos/
khor tu bap pe rab chags bu dug tang/
ri dag nu tang nas pang Tsering gyur/
te tag vang pa de va la/
neg pa gang cig tsering nam tug ces/
dag pe thin yig chog ca kya ga ma yi/
khur chas snyams par zes pe gyan tu cin/
pag yot sod nam sam skyet pe/
nam pa tham cat khen pe jugs ku lha/
zogs par na ve tashis stag gyat ki
zug nyan spang zugs sarpe lang cho can/
di dag gang gis khim tu da cet na/
chi met chet tang nave met pa de/
ga tang gut pa met lang the stop/
mi zang sod nam phung pe phel gyur/
chi tang nang gi thunpa meng pe chogs
zom pe nyen po chog tang di yin jes/

chos kun ten cing del var jung ve thul/
ses nas sma va mang pos chi tu ling/
ge legs shes pe chon ri sa mig ki ji/
kot pe ten zung ge ve kha nyam ki/
lus yan che yi jon jing gyas pe thod/
de ji das du yur du za var shok/
de dag ma sun cot pa nir snags nas/
cams pe jum dungs kar pos su jin tu/
de dang ge ve dud ci tag thung pe/
ta shis tampe sa tangs gyan gyur cig/
te tar nas khang gang du ta shis pe ten del du/
de var aos pe cheni nam la dub tang/
tashis stags gyat ki jug nyan nam par got pa la/
nye var kho var shat pa chig su cang va/
di yang do dagma va bande sulthim rin chen gyis/
palde ge lhun dup stop chos dar this pa vo
Manglam Tashis
- -
- -
nang zan legs lam got pa mot lam/
- - - - - ganga lam sum gyu yang nyes skyot dam/
ri sil -
jod pe zil mang cet/
ka shi li yul dag gyal pos sungs pe chogs/
nag chat tug po jig tu lang chen tel/
ri bong gong ma set te sog that pe/
jung vaphan thun yik chukas za var nas/

TRANSLATION

The inscription is written from the wall in front of the lhun grub khang door. It was very difficult for me to write down Tibetan inscription from the wall. However, I had made all possible precautions while writing the same.

The inscription was written in seven rows (or lines), each line was having 4'10" in length. The whole, inscription was written in 4'6" wide and 4'10" in length. The translation of the inscription is as under]:

> When the world was emerging, Maha Cini, a beautiful and lonly place was developed. A great sidddha then came. In those days in front of the mountain a beautiful lake was situated. The water from that lake irrigate the valleys surrounded the mountain. The lush green, fruits and flowers as a result decorated the region. Thanks to Buddhisattva[1] and Siddha who always ready to help all sentient beings and did welfare works for them. The animals and birds without any hesitation walked nearby, and loved Siddha.
>
> *Shava's* life as a result increased considerably. This all happened due to non-violence. Thus the above natural things of long life are named in general as Tsering Namtuk.[2]
>
> Therefore, to see the paintings of Tsering Nantuk enlarge the heart of those human beings who do right works. Their body thereafter shine by eight auspicious signes.
>
> They live long and their life free from all diseases.
>
> Under such condition they do not feel weak, old and remain young for long time.
>
> They as a matter of facts will get prosperity by removing inside and outside obstructions.
>
> The eight auspicious signs[3] remove the evil spirits and demons effects. Thus their knowledge increases, they are honoured literily, by infine *Puniya* and *Vidhyas* human beings life longevity increase like tree. The fruit of *De zee* leads us towards prosperity.
>
> By following *Maitta* and love ways every one gets happiness and *puniya* in life.
>
> The auspicious eight signs by way of *pratitsampudapada* Tsering Namtuk represents the long life of six things as depicted on wall.
>
> The poem deals with those auspicious symbols should be written on every religions institutions.

By doing this human being will get *punya* and prosperity by lama Tsulthim Pinchen.

NOTES AND REFERENCES

1. Bodhisattva: The concept of the Bodhisattva is "Enlightenment being" and is especially decisive for the character of the Mahayana. The Enlightenment requires not only the cessation of ignorance but also the exercise of compassion to work for the liberation of all sentient beings. He after attaining enlightenment, voluntarily remains in the world in order to work, by preaching and activity, for the deliverance of all. Cf Finegan Jack: *Tibet: A Dreamt of Image,* Tibet House, New Delhi, 1986: 68.
2. Tsering Namtuk: Tib. tse ring rnam drug. They are six in number as listed below:
   (i) brag tshe ring
   (ii) chu tshe ring
   (iii) shing tshe ring
   (iv) mi tshe ring
   (v) bya tshe ring
   (vi) ri dvag tshe ring.
3. The eight auspicious signs: Here follows the details of auspicious signs:
   (i) *Swastika:* Tib. gyung drug, auspicious symbol of great antiquity, is in its form with the arms turned to the right a sign of the Buddha and often appears in place of the wheel.
   (ii) Sword: Tib. ral gri; khadga; is the symbol of understanding which cuts through ignorance; accordingly it is especially the emblem of Manjusri; holds sword in his right hand, or it rises out of a lotus blossom.
   (iii) Vajra: Tib. rdo-rje Pron. dorje. As a visible object the dorje may appear as a stylized thunderbolt, with rays at either end, or as a nucleus from which on either side emerges a lotus blossom. The double dorje is especially the attribute of the Bodhisattva Amoghasiddhi and of Tara his consort. When dorje and bell together used by the deity, this symbolises as male and female elements. The dorje is the male element stands for *upaya* and bell stands for *prajna,* in the combination of these two which is necessary for enlightenment.

(iv) Rosary: It consists 108 bits of sandal wood and other matter; counting mantra through bits helps to remove ignorance.

(v) Kartarrka: It is the symbol to destroy ignorance.

(vi) Phurba: It is used in removing the influence of evil spirits

(vii) Axe: It is the symbol to cut the sin of attachment.

(viii) Damaru: It is used during prayer.

29

Religious Pothis in the Library of Matho Monastery

Matho monastery has a good collection of Buddhist texts (or pothis). These are listed below:

1.	Kangyur (Tib. bk'a 'agyur)	102 Volumes
2.	Sakya ka bum (Tib. sa skya bk'a- 'abum)	15 Volumes
3.	Norchen ka bum (Tib. ngor chen bk'a - abum)	04 Volumes
4.	Lam das lar gyud ki-nam thar (Tib. lam 'abras-blab rgyud kyi rnam thar)	03 Volumes
5.	Mani ka bum (Tib. ma ni bk'a 'abum	02 Volumes
6.	Beurya kar po stot cha (Tib. be durya dkar postot cha)	01 Volume
7.	Beurya kar po smad cha (Tib. be durya kar po smad cha)	01 Volume
8.	Beurya ya sel stot cha (Tib. be durya gy'a sel stot cha)	01 Volume
9.	Beurya ya sel smad cha (Tib. be durya gy'a sel smad cha)	02 Volumes
10.	Stan gyur gyi kar chag (Tib. bstan 'agyur gyid kar chag)	01 Volume
11.	Ti med sel gong (Tib. dri med shel gong)	01 Volume
12.	Ti med shel theng (Tib. dri med shel phreng)	01 Volume
13.	Lama Sangyas gyaltsen gyi zadnam (Tib. bla ma sngs rgyas rgyal tsangyi mdzad nam)	01 Volume
14.	Lama marpa tang mile dzad nam (Tib. bla ma mar pa dang mi l'ai mdzad nam)	01 Volume
15.	Lhan thap (Tib. lhan thabs)	01 Volume

16. Sung ngag khog phug (Tib. gsung ngag khog phug) — 01 Volume
17. nga vang chos gyal gyi nam thar (Tib. dga dbang chos rgyal gyi-rnam thar) — 01 Volume
18. De chog chos jung tang cham jor (Tib. bde mchog chos 'abyung-dang mtsams sbyor — 01 Volume
19. Phur pa ka thong sogs (Tib. phur pa bk'a thong sogs — 01 Volume
20. Sangs chang kun ga sod nam kyi stod jod (Tib. snags 'achang kun'dg'a bstod nams kyi rtogs brjod) — 01 Volume
21. Sangs chang kung ga tashis kyi nam thar — 01 Volume
22. Pal sakye dung rab chen mo (Tib. dpal sa sky'ai gdung rabs — 01 Volume
23. ka dam bu chos (Tib bk'a gdams bu chos) — 01 Volume
24. Sang dus jam dur gyi stot pa (Tib. gsang 'adus 'ajam rdor gyi bstod pa) — 01 Volume
25. Jam dor can ras zig kyi-dub kyi mida ve-khyad par (Tib. 'ajam rdor spyan ras gzigs kyi sgrub dkyil mi 'adra b'ai khyad par) — 01 Volume
26. Jam dor kyil chog (Tib. 'jam rdor dkyil chog) — 01 Volume
27. Jigjet dub thab (Tib. 'ajigas byed sgrub thabs) — 01 Volume
28. Tam pa chos phags yul tu tar thul (Tib. dam p'ai chos 'aphags yul du dar tsul) — 01 Volume
29. Gyud gyal shing ji shed kyi chos jung (Tib. rgyud rgyal gshin rje gshid kyi chos 'abyung) — 01 Volume
30. Sapan kunga gyalsan gyi jadnam (Tib. sa pan kun dg'a rgyal mtsan gyi mdzad rnam) — 01 Volume
31. Jo vo ji zad nam kadam leg bam (Tib. jobo rje'ai mdzad rnam bk'a gdams glegs bam — 01 Volume
32. Ser Od dam pa (Tib. gse 'aod dam pa) — 01 Volume
33. Sang chan Kun ga rin chen-gyi nam thar (Tib. sngags 'achad kun dg'a rin chen gyi rnam thar — 01 Volume
34. Kye dor dub thaps za zer (Tib. kye rdor sagub thabs zla zer) — 01 Volume
35. Jigjet dub thab (Tib. 'ajigs byed sgrub thabs) — 01 Volume
36. Dolkar gyi cin sreg (Tib. Csgrol dkar gyi sbyin sreg) — 01 Volume

37. Gyu tag nis kyi nam shad
(Tib. rgyu brtag gnyis kyi rnam mshad) 01 Volume
38. Sang dus lha cu gui dub thabs nyi od (Tib. gsang 'adus lha bcu dgu'ai sgrub thabs nyi 'aod) 01 Volume
39. Sang dus zam pe kyil chog
(Tib. gsang 'adus 'ajam p'ai dkyil chog) 01 Volume
40. Sang dus tor chog (Tib. gsang 'adus gtor chog) 01 Volume
41. Sang dus chod thed
(Tib. gsang 'adus mchod phred) 01 Volume
42. Sang dus dor jei stot pa
(Tib. gsang 'adus rdo-rje 'ai bstod pa) 01 Volume
43. Sang dus lhan thaps
(Tib. gsang 'adus lhan thabas) 01 Volume
44. Kha sang ve go ched
(Tib. mkh'a gsang b'ai go byed) 01 Volume
45. Jam gon Tashis lhun dup kyi sku stot
(Tib. 'ajam mgon bkris lhun grub kyi sku bstod) 01 Volume
46. Can ra zigs kyi cin sreg
(Tib. sbyan res gzigs kyi sbyin sreg) 01 Volume
47. Na ro kha hod kyi dup thaps
(Tib. na ro mkh'a spyod kyi sgrub thabs) 01 Volume
48. mkha chot me zin srek
(Tib. mkh'a spyod m'ai sbyin-sreg) 01 Volume
49. Vir sung bu chogs (Tib. Vir srung dpu phyogs) 01 Volume
50. Sine je shed lha ngai dub thabs
(Tib. gshin rje gshed lha lng'ai - sgrub thabs) 01 Volume
51. Shin je shad mar lha ngi kyil khor gi cho ga
(Tib. gshin rje gshed dmar lha lng'ai dkyil 'akhor gyi cho ga) 01 Volume
52. Sin ji shed kyi cin sreg
(Tib. gshin rje gshed kyi-sbyin sreg) 01 Volume
53. Pal sa skyai ka sung nam kyi stod chogs (Tib. dpal sa skya'ai bk'a srung rnams kyi bstod tsogs) 01 Volume
54. Tasis pod (Tib bkris pod) 01 Volume
55. Dolme kil chog (Tib sgrol m'ai ngkyil chog) 01 Volume
56. Stag nis nam shad (Tib. brtag gnyis rnams-shad) 01 Volume

57. ca gyud ki nam shad (Tib. bya rgyud kyi rnam bshad) — 01 Volume
58. Ke dor gi ked rim za zer (Tib. kye rdor gyi bskyed rim zla zer) — 01 Volume
59. Gyu tus ki vang gi togs pa kye ve rim pa (Tib. rgyu nyus kyi dbang gi rtogs pa skye b'ai rim pa) — 01 Volume
60. Tag nis ka del (Tib. brtag gnis dk'a 'agrel) — 01 Volume
61. Jigs cet ra lungs ki gya cher del pa (Tib. 'ajigs byed ra lugs kyi rgya cher 'agrel pa) — 01 Volume
62. Chot gyut ki nam shad (Tib. sbyod rgyud kyi rnam bshad) — 01 Volume
63. Do de kal zang (Tib. mdo sde bskal-bzang) — 01 Volume
64. Gya tong pa (Tib. brgyad stong pa) — 01 Volume
65. Da tog ser sum (Tib. sgra tog gser gsum) — 01 Volume
66. Sung nag khog phup (Tib. gsung ngag khog phub) — 01 Volume
67. Nor chen do je chang gi nam thar (Tib. ngor chen rdorje 'achang gi rnam mthar) — 01 Volume
68. Be sngon (Tib. be sngon) — 01 Volume
69. De chog chos jung tang cham jor cas la (Tib. bde mchog chos 'abyung dang mtsans sbyor bcas la) — 01 Volume
70. Ges pa Dor jei gyung (Tib. ngges pa rdo rje'ai rgyung) — 01 Volume
71. Do than na chogs (Tib. mdo phran sna tsogs) — 01 Volume
72. Gya ton pa sum phap (Tib. brgyad stong pa gsum phab) — 01 Volume
73. Bum (Tib. 'abum) — 01 Volume
74. Go rab jams pa sod nams (Tib. go rab 'abyams pa bsod nams)
75. Senggei sung bum (Tib. sengge'ai gsung 'abum) — 12 Volumes
76. Dup Taps kun dus (sgrub thams kun btus) — 14 Volumes
77. Dor khang chen pal dan chos kyong gi nam thar (Tib. dor mkhan chen dpal ldan chos skyong gi - rnam thar) — 04 Volumes
78. Cang thor gon po (Tib. gtsang gtor mgon po) — 02 Volumes
79. Be tur ya sel (Tib. be turya gy'a sel) — 02 Volumes

80.	Kangyur (Tib. bk'a 'agyur)	103 Volumes
81.	Stangyur (bstan 'agyur)	Complete set of Volumes

NOTE AND REFERENCE

1. Jamyang Gyaltsan (ed.): *The History of Ladakh Monasteries,* All Ladakh Gonpa Society, Leh-Ladakh; 1995: 476-'80.

30

Branches of Matho Monastery

Matho monastery does not have many branch gonpas. The possible reasons may be as follows:

1. During 15th century Tungpa Dorje Palzang[1] visited Ladakh. Later went to Matho for meditation. He was called by king Dragspa Bumde[2] for *Rabnas* of Tesru chorten. On the king's request he performed Rabnas ceremony in an amicable manner. Subsequently he established Matho monastery on the present site. He passed his maximum time in Matho and its nearby area, but did not propagate his sect tradition in the other parts of Ladakh.
2. During king Jamyang Namgyal[3] period Baltis invaded Ladakh. King recruited maximum Lamas from Matho monastery in Ladakh Army in order to defend his kingdom from enemy. Balti defeated Ladakh Army in all fronts. King was sent to Skardu Jail. Later he was released under the condition that he would marry with Gyal Khatun[4] and helped to propagate Islam. Jamyang Namgyal after marriage with Gyal Khatun came to Ladakh and again became the king of Ladakh. Matho monastery on the other hand was almost destroyed by Balti Army. The head lama of this monastery requested king to re-establish the monastery and repair the temples. King promised to do so. But he died soon. Later his son Singge Namgyal[5] became Ladakh King. He was influenced by stag-tsang ras-pa[6] of Drug-pa K'agyud tradition lama. He was a great Siddha. King appointed him as Raj Guru.[7] On his

advice he helped in the propogation of Drug-pa tradition throughout the Ladakh. As a result Sakya tradition Matho monastery renovation works was neglected. Consequently, lama population also decreased considerably. Since then no head lama of Sakya tradition payed his attention for strengthening the monastic tradition. This time Matho monastery is looked after by Gonpa Welfare Society. But the absence of head lama in this monastery is a great concern.

Besides above facts, the monastery has the following branch gonpas in which it deputes one pujari (Tib. Komner) for every three years tenure.[8]

1. Skidmang
2. Igugurgon
3. Lehgurgon
4. Gogmin

Skidmang (Tib. Skyid Mang Dgon Pa)

This gonpa is situated in Rong side. It was possibly built during 15th century A.D. Though it does not have good lama strength, lookafter by Mang gon shesrigde don chogs pa rogs (Tib. many dgon shes rig bde don tsot pai rogs).[9]

Igugurgon (Tib. 'ai Gur Mgon)

This gonpa is named after village Igu (Tib. 'aigu) means a village which has nine shapes. This gonpa has one Gurgon (Tib. gur mgon) gonpo in a ferocious form and Buddha statue made of bronze or brass. Besides there are many small buddha statues. In every three years gap Matho monastery depute one pujari lama to perform rituals and daily prayer at the gonpa.[10]

Lehgurgon (Tib. Gle'ai Gur Mgon)

This Temple is in Leh and has following statues:[11]

1. *Kurgon (Tib. gur mgon mgonpo):* He is a famous gonpo and treated as a powerful Buddhist deity. The statue of Kurgon is made of sandalwood.
2. *Buddha: Height:* 6'- to 7'

Metal: Brass or Bronze

Matho monastery depute one Lama pujari in every three years gap. He looks after the temple and performs daily prayer.

Gogmin Lhakhang

It is said that Matho monastery has one branch gonpa at Spiti area in Himachal Pradesh. This gonpa is known as Gogmin (Tib. gog min dgon bzes).[12] It is very far away from Ladakh therefore, does not have cultural relations with Matho monastery. Due to this reason the monastery does not depute Lama pujari there.

NOTES AND REFERENCES

1. Tungpa Dorje Palzang: He was the famous lama of Sakya tradition of Mahayana Buddhism, arrived Ladakh during 15th century and established a temple of his order in Matho village, near Leh. The same was later developed as Matho monastery.
2. King Dragspa Bumde: He was the religious King of Ladakh during 15th Century A.D. He erected many religious buildings viz. Namgyal tsemo temple, spituk monastery etc.
3. King Jamyang Namgyal: After the death of king Tsewang Namgyal, his younger brother Jamyang Namgyal became the king of Ladakh during 16th century A.D. During his reign Balti war took place. King Jamyang Namgyal was defeated, later was released when he married Ali Mir's daughter Gyal Khatun.
4. Gyal Khatun: She was the daughter of Ali Mir Sher Khan, and was married with King Jamyang Namgyal with a mission to propogate Islam in Ladakh quietly.
5. Singge Namgyal: He was the son of Jamyang Namgyal and Gyal Khatun, and had inherited the warlike spirit of his grandfather, Ali Mir. He was married to Rupshu princess Skalzang. Cf. A.H. Francke, *'A History of Western Tibet'*, Asian Educational Services, New Delhi; 1995 (Printed): 96.
6. Stag-tsang-ras-pa: He was a great Siddha, king Singge Namgyal invited him in his kingdom. He visited many Buddhist religious centres in India and had seen all the important eighty saints face to face. later introduced Mani-well building tradition in Ladakh.
7. Raj-Guru: King Singge Namgyal when invited stag-tsang-ras-pa, honoured him as Raj Guru.

8. Jamyang Gyaltsan (ed.): *The History of Ladakh Monasteries*, All Ladakh Gonpa Society, Leh-Ladakh, 1995, p. 481.
9. *Ibid.*
10. *Ibid.*
11. *Ibid.*
12. *Ibid.*, pp. 481-482.

Bibliography

Gordon, Antoinettek: 'The Iconography of Tibetan Lamaism,' Munshiram Manoharlal Pub. Pvt. Ltd., New Delhi, 1998.

Francke, A.H.: 'A History of Western Tibet,' Asian Educational Services, New Delhi, 1995.

Fredric, W.: 'An Encyclopaedia of Buddhist Deities, Demigods, Godlings, Saints and Demons,' Vol. I, D.K. Print World Pvt. Ltd., New Delhi, 1994.

Finegan, Jack: 'Tibet A Dreamt of Image,' Tibet House, New Delhi, 1986.

Jamyang Gyaltsan (ed.): 'The History of Ladakh Monasteries,' All Ladakh Gonpa Society, Leh-Ladakh; 1995.

Jamyang Gyaltsan: 'Mangtri Monastery', Cultural and Welfare Society Mangtre Gonpa, Leh, 2005.

Jina, Prem Singh: 'Ladakh Aur Paryatan' C Tourism in Ladakh), In: Ist National Conference, CIBS, Leh-Ladakh, 1981.

Jina, Prem Singh: 'Ladakh Ki Sanskriti Per Seemant Sanskriti ka Prabhav' News Latter, New Delhi, Sept.-Oct., 1982.

Jina, Prem Singh: 'Is Samaye Bhagwan Buddha Kaha Hai', Dinman, Vol. 18, 28th Nov.-4th Dec., 1982:46.

Jina, Prem Singh: 'Santi stupa Ladakh ke', Yojana, Jammu, March, 1983: 15-16.

Jina, Prem Singh: 'Seet Kal Me Leh Ghati,' Seraja, Jammu-65. March, 1983.

Jina, Prem Singh: 'Boudh Biksus of Ladakh,' In Proceed of All India Conference, Delhi Univ., Delhi, 1983.

Jina, Prem Singh: 'A Brief Introduction of Ladakh Gonpas: In Ladakh Life and Culture,' Centre for Centre Asian Studies, Kashmir Univ. Srinagar, 1986.

Jina, Prem Singh: 'A Survey of Buddhist Community in Ladakh Himalaya,'

In 12 International Buddhist Conference, Both Gaya, Vol. XII, 1986.

Jina, Prem Singh: 'Tourism in Ladakh Himalaya,' Indus Pub. Co., New Delhi, 1994.

Jina, Prem Singh: 'High Pasturelands of Ladakh Himalaya', Indus Pub. Co., New Delhi, 1995.

Jina, Prem Singh: 'Phyang Monastery of Ladakh,' Indus Pub. Co., New Delhi, 1995.

Jina, Prem Singh: 'Famous Western Explorers to Ladakh,' Indus Pub. Co., New Delhi, 1995.

Jina, Prem Singh: 'Ladakh: The Land and the People', Indus Pub. Co., New Delhi, 1996.

Jina, Prem Singh (ed.): Recent Researchers on the Himalaya, Indus Pub. Co., New Delhi, 1997.

Jina, Prem Singh: Tibetan Manuscripts and Inscriptions of Ladakh Himalayas,' Satguru Pub., New Delhi, 1998.

Jina, Prem Singh and Konckok Namgyal: 'Lamayuru Monastery of Ladakh Himalaya', Om Pub. New Delhi, 1999.

Jina, Prem Singh: 'Some Monasteries of Drigung pa Order in Central Ladakh,' Satguru Pub., New Delhi, 1999.

Jina, Prem Singh: 'Changing Face of Ladakh,' Om Pub. Co., New Delhi, 1999.

Jina, Prem Singh: 'Ladakh Past and Present,' Gyan Pub., New Delhi, 2000.

Jina, Prem Singh (ed.) 'Religious History of Ladakh,' Satguru Pub., New Delhi, 2001.

Jina, Prem Singh: 'Ladakh Ki Kala Avam Sanskriti,' IGNCA, New Delhi, 2001.

Jina, Prem Singh and A.H. Francke: 'First Hand Tibetan Inscriptions on Rock and Stone from Ladakh Himalaya,' Satguru Pub., New Delhi, 2003.

Jina, Prem Singh: 'Ladakh Himalaya: Past and Present,' Anmol Pub., New Delhi.

Jina, Prem Singh: 'Tourism and Buddhist Monasteries of Ladakh,' Gyan Pub. New Delhi, 2007.

Jina, Prem Singh: 'Ladakh: Culture and Tradition,' Gyan Pub., New Delhi, 2007.

Jina, Prem Singh: 'Buddhism Beyond Zojila, Sakshi Pub., New Delhi, 2008.

Jina, Prem Singh: 'Buddhism and Environment,' In: International Buddhist Conference, Japanese Temple, Bodh Gaya, 2007.

Jina, Prem Singh: 'Buddhism in Lahul,' Sri Satguru Pub., New Delhi, (In Press).

Index

K

L

M

N

O

P

Z